GETTING THE DEAL Done

Tips & Strategies to Get Your Business Buy-Sell Deal Done — Successfully

John Martinka, The Escape Artist®

WITH CONTRIBUTIONS FROM 11 OTHER DEAL PROFESSIONALS

Contents

Preface

Getting the Deal Done is my fourth book. Here's a short summary of the others:

- My first book, *Buying a Business That Makes You Rich; Toss Your Job, Not the Dice,* concerns what it takes to successfully locate, analyze and structure an acquisition. The target audience is the executive making the leap from corporate employment to business ownership. The book is now in its second edition.

- *If They Can Sell Pet Rocks, Why Can't You Sell Your Business (For What You Want)?* is a roadmap for owners covering the steps necessary to sell a business with style, grace, and more money.

- *Company Growth By Acquisition Makes Dollars & Sense* is for the business owner wanting to make a jump versus relying solely on organic growth. At the end are 19 reasons why you should consider growth by acquisition, which are reprised in *Getting the Deal Done.*

Within all of the strategies and tactics for closing a deal, what often gets lost in books like mine and others are the little nuances that get the deal done, and all of the things that prevent the deal from closing. This book is different from others on this subject, as each chapter (most are about 500 words) contains a concise explanation of proven techniques to use, actions to avoid, and tips on overcoming obstacles as you work toward *Getting the Deal Done.*

This book also includes numerous guest chapters from other deal pros, so you may find some overlap of information—which is good, as it tells you that many consider the topic important. Thanks to the following individuals for their contributions:

- Curt Case

- Curt Maier

- Dean Altaras & Billy Poll

- Greg Russell

- Gregory Kovsky

- Jessica Martinka

- John O'Dore

- Michelle Bomberger

- Pete McDowell

- Robert Hild

- Ted Leverette

Common sense—most of these tips are just that, but it's amazing how many buyers and sellers go out of their way to avoid common sense.

This book has three parts:

1. The first third of the book is primarily for sellers, although buyers will learn a lot from this information as well. It comprises tips and strategies to make the business more attractive to buyers.

2. The second part consists of deal-making tips on search, analysis, valuation, negotiation, due diligence, transition, and closing.

3. In the final part, my rules for business-buying, exiting, and selling are interspersed among tips for all of the above. The book concludes with an extended essay on the 19 reasons to consider growth by acquisition.

The first part of the book is very important. It is estimated that only 10-20% of business owners do any kind of exit planning, because the owner is busy and, in my opinion, many owners think their business is so special it doesn't need any preparation. For those who want to exit with style, grace, and more money, pay heed to the first part. Your buyer(s) will appreciate it.

Acknowledgments

The idea for this book came in 2015, a couple of years after the first edition of *Buying A Business That Makes You Rich*. This project got sidetracked while I was writing *If They Can Sell Pet Rocks, Why Can't You Sell Your Business (For What You Want?)* and *Company Growth By Acquisition Makes Dollars & Sense*. I restarted *Getting the Deal Done* in 2018, only to realize I needed to update *Buying A Business That Makes You Rich,* given the changes that had since occurred in the market.

What drove me to action to complete this book was COVID-19. In March 2020, much of the country came to a standstill, and around April 1 I figured I would get the book cranked out pretty quick. The standstill didn't last all that long, so a two-month project became a four-month one.

My acknowledgments are to family, friends, support network, etc. I do thank all of them, especially my wife, Jan, and my daughter, Jessica, who is part of the company.

The biggest thanks go to all of my past clients, without whom I wouldn't have the experience to write this or any of my other books. And a special thanks to the 12 people who accepted my offer to contribute a chapter each. It's tough to do something like this when you're busy. So, again, thanks to (in alphabetical order by first name) Curt Case, Curt Maier, Dean Altaras & Billy Poll, Greg Russell, Gregory Kovsky, Jessica Martinka, John O'Dore, Michelle Bomberger, Pete McDowell, Robert Hild, and Ted Leverette. You'll find their contact information at the end of their respective chapters.

Chapter 1

Know the Process (and What's Most Important)

Buyers and sellers have a similar process that involves:

1. Preparation
2. Search and screening
3. Finance
4. Analyze
5. Value and pricing
6. Deal making
7. Negotiation
8. Due diligence
9. Transition planning
10. Closing

When it comes to executing the process, Point 2—search and screening—is *the* most important step on the way to success, whether you're a buyer or a seller.

Why? Because you can be the best negotiator, the best dealmaker, or an absolute superstar at uncovering issues and hidden gems in a company (due diligence), but those skills are useless if you have no business to evaluate or buyer with whom to negotiate.

Searching is a contact sport. The more contacts you make, the better your chance of success. But before you put on your shoulder pads and go hit the streets, take a step back. Search actually starts with preparation. For sellers, it's thinking about and identifying your logical buyer. Is it:

1. An executive escaping the corporate world (a corporate refugee)?

2. Another small business?

3. A private equity group?

4. A larger company?

A business doing $2 million in sales is almost never going to sell to the latter two buyer types. A business doing $20 million or more will rarely sell to the first two.

Chasing the wrong buyer type because your best friend sold to that type of buyer would have you chasing your tail and becoming incredibly frustrated. Once you identify the logical buyer, you can prepare the company in a way that emphasizes its strengths so it appeals to those buyers.

For example, if your logical buyer is an individual (a financial buyer needing a salary, profits, etc.), you will want a business in which the buyer can step into the role of CEO with a good team underneath her. If your logical buyer is a private equity group or large company, you'll want to have a top-notch management team, which may or may not include you. These buyers want a management team in place and will pay for it.

For buyers, it's taking time to think through your criteria—not just general industries, say, manufacturing or restaurant—and asking questions including, but not limited to:

- How is the market of the business doing?

- What does the owner do daily, weekly, monthly?

- What do *you* want to do once you own the business?

- What type of employees (white-collar, blue-collar, low-skilled) does the business have?

- Where is it located?

- Who does the firm sell to (consumer or business)?

Here is a list of very common business traits buyers seek:

- Profitable company

- Defensible position

- Sustainable product advantage

- High margins

- Scalable

- Proprietary product or service

- Not trendy

The point is, the answers to the above can be found in many, many types of businesses. And if buyers know what they want, almost any industry can have firms that will fit the bill.

See the Big Picture

Many years ago, I consulted to a business owner who ran a production shop. It was a fairly simple operation; the machine was programed, the parts fed into the machine, the output sorted and sent on to the shipping department.

The problem was, the owner was the only person who could program the machine, and he wouldn't train anybody else to program it. He had all kinds of excuses, the "best" one being: it took 20 minutes for him to program it, and it would take an hour for him to teach someone else how to do it, so he kept on programing while his employees sat around playing on their phones.

This isn't isolated. I recently met with an owner who spent 10-15 minutes talking about what he does on daily, weekly and monthly, and the bottom line was he filled his weeks (and weekends) doing menial tasks a $10-to-$15-per-hour person could easily do. He went into great detail about an incident with an employee pressure-washing something, and it became clear his frustration could easily have been avoided had he given the employee three minutes of direction. But if it was done correctly, what would he have to complain about?

Are you a micromanager? If so, get over it if you want to get your deal done smoothly and in a timely manner. Good examples of micromanaging include:

- **Working on the legal agreements without your attorney.** One seller put his attorney on hold and took over the review and negotiation of the purchase-and-sale agreement (PSA), even though he didn't understand the little legal nuances. He concluded that the other side was trying to pull a fast one on him; only when convinced to reengage his attorney did he find out it was standard legal terminology. It ended up costing him and the buyer more time, energy and legal fees.

- **Worrying about dollars, not thousands of dollars.** This hits buyers and sellers equally. One buyer got caught up in staffing issues of about $10,000, which distracted him from the big picture worth 10-20 times that annually. Sellers will stress over the tax difference of the non-compete agreement being allocated at $10,000 vs. $5,000 on a seven-figure deal. (Sellers pay ordinary income tax, not capital gains, on the non-compete.)

- **Fretting about the interest rate (say, a .125% difference).** Instead, focus on whether that bank can get the loan approved, can meet deadlines, and will be a good partner going forward.

Another thing (mostly) sellers do is nibble. Once the deal is agreed upon, they keep coming back for more. They often don't notice they're doing it, but the buyer does, and gets extremely frustrated. Often this relates to what assets will be left in company. Sellers tend to come back for a little more, whether it's the working capital formula, the work-in-progress, or certain assets.

Tip: Getting the deal done means seeing the big picture. A lot of things can get in the way of a deal closing, and the more delays—especially annoying little ones—the greater the chance the deal will become unraveled.

Sellers: The First Three Questions to Ask Yourself (and more)

Let's assume you are selling for reasons other than a catastrophic event. You may be retiring, getting burned out, or just ready to seek your next great adventure in life. You must pay attention to the "softer" issues. They are much more important than the hard facts of having an exit plan or actually selling your business. These issues aren't usually involved in a sale forced by a catastrophic event.

Selling your business is an emotional rollercoaster. Don't ignore this, or it will hit you upside the head like a linebacker at full speed colliding with a wide receiver. Realize that the 800-pound gorilla in the room is the question, "Are *you* ready to sell?" Seller remorse hits when you realize you got caught up in the moment and can't fathom not going into the business (your baby) every day. If you're coasting because you can't bear the thought of leaving, realize:

Value decreases as the owner gets burned out.

I tell business buyers to approach an acquisition with the understanding that it's a five-to-ten-year engagement and investment. If you end up falling in love with it, great. But don't look for the perfect business you'll be married to forever. Understand that at some time you will leave the business, and it's your decision if you leave by dying at your desk at age 90 or selling when the time is right.

I do a lot of handholding as we glide through this life-changing event, which is the largest financial transaction of sellers' lives, much larger than the value of their home. It's important to take time to think and talk through these issues. You must make the effort to understand and deal with it, so you make the right decision for your family and you.

First question: *If the big question is "Are you ready to sell?" then an even bigger question might be, "Is your spouse ready to sell?"* Here's an example: My client was two months or more into the selling process. He'd had a valuation done on the business. We had packaged information about the company and had received an outline of an offer. He then said, "I guess I'd better talk to my wife about this." Boom! The process came to a screeching halt, and his wife felt betrayed that he hadn't discussed selling with her. (The buyer and I had both heard from the seller that all was OK with his wife regarding selling.)

Once she calmed down, her next issue was that she didn't want him around the house all the time. That issue was (somewhat) solved when he reminded her that he hadn't been going into the business every day for quite a while, and with a new general manager on board he would be around more than ever. ("So get used to it, honey.")

No matter what the size of your company, no matter what your age or situation—consult with your spouse first and make him or her part of the process.

Second question: *How much money is enough?* Your financial planner is a valuable member of your team. Know what you need financially. If you're retiring, do you need money from the sale to supplement your other assets and income? Do you need enough money to buy or start another business?

In any event, work with your investment advisor so you have a clear picture of your goals and capacities. The only thing worse than finding out during the selling process that the proceeds aren't enough for what you want to do is finding out post-sale that you are short the necessary funds. Get detailed projections, including the probability of your assets lasting well past your spouse's and your life expectancy based on various investment strategies.

And remember, projections are only estimates based on a series of assumptions. They are not a guarantee and need to be monitored. Evaluating your personal situation well in advance allows you to get a business valuation and prepare the business to meet your financial requirements

Third question: *What will you do, and if it's retirement you want, does your spouse want you around the house 24/7?* The seller who has a plan of varied activities post-sale comes across as a lot more serious about selling compared to the owner with no plan. Take some time to think about this, discuss it with family, and know what you're going to do. There used to be a story (true or not, I don't know) about all of the Boeing people who retired at 65 and died at 67 or 68 because their lives had changed so dramatically. Social Security was designed with a retirement age of 65, because in the 1930s life expectancy for men at 65 was about 68.

Don't let your business be your life. It should be a component of your life that gives your life meaning and provides you with a lifestyle.

Do you care about your children and employees and what will happen to them post-sale? If one or more of your children are active in the business, you need to decide what happens to them if you sell to an outside buyer. You might want to consider selling to your children. It can't be a sentimental decision; your children must be qualified to run the business and pay you for it.

An upcoming chapter mentions the son who was a shop foreman and ran the business into the ground. Another owner told me he was upset because neither his son nor his daughter wanted to take over his business. I asked what his children did, and he replied that one was a lawyer and the other was a doctor. You'd think he'd be proud, not disappointed.

The same goes for your loyal employees, especially your management. Do they have the guts to buy the business? Do they have the money? Are they willing to sign a personal guarantee and put up personal collateral to the bank?

One final word on this: Work with your attorney, family, and life insurance agent in advance if you have one or more children active in the business and one or more not active there. It can be done, but it takes planning to make sure all are treated fairly. Those active in the business won't want to work hard to have dividends go to their siblings, and those not active will feel slighted if you favor those children working in the business (especially if the business is the vast majority of your net worth).

Chapter 4

20 Rules of Business Exiting & Selling

1. Searching for a buyer is sales. It's the same as when you prospect for customers. There has to be a good fit, and the buyer must add value (as you do for your customers). It's all about finding the right buyer.

2. Cash is king; and so is cash flow. The more cash flow you have, the higher your price, and the more cash you'll get at closing.

3. The queen is relationships, and, as in chess, the queen is the most powerful piece in the game. It's a relationship game, and don't forget it. Nobody buys from or sells to someone they don't like.

4. It's not what you get; it's what you keep. Pay attention to taxes, terms, and structure.

5. Watch out for dependencies in the business. The first place a buyer looks for dependencies is to the owner. How dependent is the business on you?

6. You must show confidence, speed and creativity. Also demonstrate constant innovation.

7. Growth hides a lot of operational warts, and those warts tend to work their way out.

8. Structure your business so the buyer falls in love with the business model and its value proposition, not just the product. This means, build a business with a defensible competitive advantage, and consider how you can leverage your competitive advantage to grow.

9. The bigger the spreadsheet, the less chance of a deal. Don't let the buyer get analysis-paralysis.

10. There are no perfect deals, so don't get emotional just because the deal isn't perfect. Emotions cause more angst than anything else. It may be a "business" deal, but buyers and sellers can get very emotional about how successful or unsuccessful the deal could be.

11. What makes you a good business owner can make you a bad deal person. Apply your high standards of business ethics and efficiency to your dealing.

12. Terms are often more important than price.

13. Don't fall for valuation traps and simplistic formulas. Don't believe that, just because a $400 million company sold for 10X EBITDA, your small business will also sell in that range.

14. Due diligence is for proving what you've told the buyer during analysis; it is no time for surprises. Don't forget to do due diligence on your buyer, and do it sooner vs. later.

15. Understand that the buyer and the bank will be "nosy" and the administrivia near closing will drive you nuts but must be done.

16. Have a great advisory team, and use them well. Don't try to do legal, tax or related work yourself. It's not worth it, and you're likely to make mistakes, which can come back to haunt you.

17. Don't let your buyer get over-leveraged. Too much debt will come back to haunt the buyer and you.

18. You both will make a leap of faith. Do it right, and that leap will be off a chair, not the roof.

19. The only thing worse than no deal is a bad deal. Be patient, and make sure the buyer is a great match.

20. Don't run a lifestyle business, i.e., don't blend your business and personal checkbooks. Take some time, prepare the finances and marketing and all of your systems, and you'll maximize value.

It's Not Like Buying or Selling a House

When someone decides to sell their house, what are the first things they do? They paint it, clean it up, get rid of clutter, fix everything, and make it as appealing as possible. Then they put up a sign, open the doors, and invite the world to come in and take a look. The more, the merrier.

Yet too few sellers properly prepare their businesses for sale (which is why I wrote *If They Can Sell Pet Rocks, Why Can't You Sell Your Business (For What You Want)?*) Sometimes a business, too, needs cleaning and painting. Often the accounting needs work, growth proved, and dependencies removed.

Recently I visited an industrial business. As we walked out, I commented to my associate, "I understand why the employees eat lunch in their cars." The offices, and especially the lunchroom, were disgustingly filthy. I wouldn't want to eat in there, that's for sure. Any buyer visiting the business would be taken aback by the conditions and wonder (remember, buyers are skeptical) if the machinery is in as bad a shape as the facilities.

So let's look at the top four things 90% of businesses need to do to increase their company's value and ultimately its price:

1. *Get the accounting systems in order.* Quit treating the business as an extension of your personal checkbook. Show lots of profit (yes, pay more tax), as buyers and banks love this.

2. *Don't just claim there's growth potential.* Take some time presale to prove it. A couple years or more of tax returns showing growth of both the top and bottom line will increase your price.

3. *Get yourself out of the day-to-day operations.* Concentrate on strategy, vision, and executing said strategy. Then make sure there are no dependencies with your employees, customers, and vendors.

4. *Show that you can attract and retain great employees.* As one of my best clients says, "A people hire A people, B people hire C people." Hire the best, and keep them around.

Buyers, there is no Multiple Listing Service for businesses. You have to prospect, call every intermediary, get referrals, and do whatever else you have to do to find a willing seller. It's not easy. In fact, it's the toughest part of the process.

And while the contract will have exhibits showing what the seller represents and warranties, it's not like buying a home, where there are legal forms the seller must fill out to disclose faults, current or historical. So it's "Buyer Beware." If you don't ask, the seller may either inadvertently or purposely not tell you things.

Finally, beauty is in the eye of the beholder, as is value. The vast majority of owners think their business is so special that traditional valuation methods don't apply to it. And you know this means they think it's worth a lot more. I recently read a "rule of thumbs" list from an old-time business broker. He stated that the true value of a business, aka the price, is halfway between what the buyer and seller think it's worth.

To compound matters, unlike homes, businesses have very few comparable sales statistics. A 3,000-square-foot house will be worth about what another 3,000-square-foot house in the same neighborhood is worth. However, two businesses in the same city and industry with the same sales and profits may be worth vastly different amounts. This could be because of any of the non-financial factors, or (as per the old appraiser joke) what if one got to their sales and profit amounts by growing 20% per year and the other by declining 20% per year?

Business Sellers Should Act Like Home Sellers

Business owners are notorious for being optimistic to the point of overconfident when they think about their business and its value. Because of this, they overwhelmingly do very little in the way of preparing it for sale.

As I write this, I'm in the midst of a deal on a very nice business. It does about $10 million in sales with 20% net if you include the new vehicles the two owners get every year or two, their spouses' vehicles, all vehicle upkeep, vacations, travel, entertainment, and deals to friends and family. The owners are still integral to the operation. Not that they do the hands-on work, but they are important to operations and customer relationships. And, like many small businesses, the accounting department is the weak little stepsister off in the corner, so information has been tough to attain in a timely or accurate way. It's called managing by checkbook, i.e., there's money in the bank, so all is good.

When the above owners were ready to sell, they were ready to sell. The switch was flipped instead of it being a dimmer switch lowered over a few years as they prepared it for sale.

Contrast this with what we all do when we sell a house. We clean it, paint it, make repairs, put a sign out front, open the doors, and invite everybody in to see and admire it. For a business, we need to do a version of cleaning and painting it.

Make the curb appeal dynamic, even if it's a dirty, oily business. The above business had stunning curb appeal. On the other end of the spectrum, remember the previous story about employees eating lunch in their cars because the lunchroom was so filthy. I wouldn't eat in it myself, and the impression a buyer will get would be the same as mine, along with the conclusion that not much attention is paid to other aspects of the business.

Preparing a business means addressing the things in the second paragraph, including but not limited to:

- Don't blend business and personal checkbooks.

- Build a team so the owner is dispensable (other than maybe being the minister of enthusiasm).

- Set up solid financial systems, enlist the right level of financial people, and keep accurate statements.

- Show that the business can grow by actually growing it, not just saying there's potential.

- Have efficient operating systems in place, and use them constantly.

- Take care of your people; they're a valuable asset.

Business owners, if you want to sell, sell for top dollar, have a happy buyer, and preserve your legacy. To make all of this possible, take time now to do the things you need to do to make your business attractive to buyers.

Above all, don't look at the above (abbreviated) list and dismiss it. Buyers like opportunity as much or more than a well-oiled machine. While all businesses have some blemishes, those with large blemishes tend to sell at a discount.

Chapter 7

Where Does the Buyer Add Value?

This is one of the most important questions buyers and sellers need to answer. It's actually the key to buyers pursuing businesses, and if they don't see how they can add value, they won't get excited. Sellers can help here by not just "selling" their company's attributes but by probing buyers to find out their skills and pointing out matches with the business.

When buyers feel they can duplicate what sellers do, they'll have interest in the businesses they are considering. When they understand that they can do what sellers do *and* add value in other areas, they get excited. I like to use the analogy of a server rack. Some slots on the rack have servers, and others are empty. If the buyer and management team fill the same slots, it's good. If they fill the existing slots and some of the empty ones, it's great, and it creates a desire to own the business.

Here is a short list of some empty "slots" buyers seek. (Most companies do many of these things correctly, but it takes only one of them to get a buyer excited.)

- **Adding marketing skills to the seller's duties.** In many companies the day-to-day marketing duties are minimal and often handled by lesser-paid employees. Many individual buyers have growth-oriented backgrounds, understand marketing, and usually understand newer marketing tactics (online marketing, social media, etc.) better than exiting owners.

- **Creating efficiencies.** For example, one buyer turned a website from a brochure to an ordering system, eliminating phone tag with customers, and improving employee productivity. He doubled the business in two years and said that creating these efficiencies was the main reason he was able to do so.

- **Improving efficiencies and processes, especially in operations.** Many good process people are out there who can make great owners, and I've seen many of them do tweaks that increase profits.

- **Providing sales, management and culture strategies**. This may include reducing order-taking and creating a culture of proactivity.

- **Just being there (a common one) as many owners get in a comfort zone and coast.** Buyers add energy, which most employees like.

I can't emphasize enough to sellers that you have to take the lead in showing opportunity if you feel the buyer is qualified to buy and grow the business. Don't just sit back and hope they get enthused. You are solving a problem the same way you solve problems for your customers. A buyer you let slip through your hands could be the best buyer you will ever meet.

This is important, because buyers are skeptical. They will look for problems, dysfunction and inefficiencies, all of which means a potentially lower price for your business. Sellers need to point out where the buyer adds value by adding emotion to the logic (of what skills the buyer has).

On the flipside, if the seller doesn't feel the buyer adds value, should she sell to him? Probably not, as the only thing worse than no buyer (or deal) is a bad buyer (or bad deal).

Chapter 8

Is the Economic Buyer Onboard?

I read a newsletter from a long-time business broker listing his "Rules of Thumb." One that caught my attention was:

"If the buyer's wife is opposed to her husband buying a business, there will be no deal. The reverse is not true; a wife will buy a business regardless of her husband's opinion."

So who is the true economic buyer? In the quote above, it's the wife, and only the wife. I've found it's easier to say it's the spouse, since I haven't seen as much evidence of wives versus husbands, as the aforementioned author has seen.

In the small business market, with an individual buyer the spouse is often called the "deal-killer." Actually, more appropriate is the term "deal-avoider." If the spouse strongly believes it's too risky to buy a business, there won't even be a search, much less a deal. If the spouse wants to limit the debt to a certain amount, it means the deal will be smaller. Usually it's phrased as, "I don't want to put the house at risk" (and banks do take home equity as collateral).

I talked to a (supposed) business buyer and asked what his wife thought of it. He hadn't talked to her yet but believed she would be fine with his decision to buy the business. I then talked to him and his potential business partner. Both of these nice chats ended with me asking about his wife. I said we would have no more calls or meetings until he dealt with the issue of getting his wife's consent. Guess what—we had no more calls or meetings.

It's just as true on the seller side. A spouse may be accustomed to a certain lifestyle, and selling the business may mean that lifestyle will change. Or perhaps the spouse does not want, in any way, shape or form, the significant other to be home 24/7. Correspondingly, the spouse may push for a sale if desiring to travel, see the spouse more, more time with grandkids, relax more at home, etc.

What about other situations?

- One business owner was funded by outside investors. He grew the business five times in less than ten years and was excited and doing well when the investors decided they needed their money out. It was time to sell. The investors were the true economic decision-makers, and this businessman decided not to use investors in his next businesses.

- Minority shareholders usually can't force a sale, other than forcing the company or majority owner to purchase the minority owner's shares. But they can cause a disruption, a major one. I worked with a founder who needed investment, became a minority owner, wanted out, didn't understand the concept of minority share discount,* and created a lot of hassle for the majority owner.

- Partnership agreements may dictate what happens when one owner wants out or wants a partner removed. This is why all partners need their own attorneys, to make sure they don't sign documents that could force them into undesired actions in the future.

In the small-to-mid-sized business market, the spouse is usually the true buyer. The spouse may not be able to say "yes" but sure can say "no."

* In the valuation world, a (steep) discount is placed on the value of minority shares in a small business. No outside market for those shares exists, and the shareholder has no real rights or ability to influence the company's direction. Thus, those shares are worth a lot less than if the company sold as a whole.

What's Your Next Great Adventure?

Buyers: Buying a business is the next great life adventure and a huge leap of faith. As I say in the preface to *Buying A Business That Makes You Rich*, buyers want to make that leap off a chair, not the roof. The question is, what business? It needs to be one for which they have the required skills to add value. It must also fit their investment criteria, and they must be able to get along very well with the seller.

A business matching the buyer's interest and skills is not the easiest thing to find. Buyers want to stay excited, and yet most don't know what type of business will excite them. Scattered buyers say, "I'll know it when I see it." They rarely see it. Overly analytical buyers want something "perfect," and of course they never see it. The successful buyer realizes it's about where they can add value, as well as not being too fussy about the exact industry.

Sellers: The real issue with this subject is, what will you, the business seller, do after you sell your business? If you can answer with a variety of activities you're planning to do, you're on the right track. This could be travel, fishing, volunteering, missionary work, starting a new business, running marathons, or just about anything else.

If you can answer with a variety of activities, and you know you're in good enough financial shape to do them based on analysis from a competent financial advisor, you're there! Advice to sellers: Don't wait until you have a deal to discuss future finance and income needs.

Recall the story about one of my clients who, six to eight weeks into the selling process, finally told his wife he was selling the company. This is what leads to a rebellion, aka divorce. Know what you want to do, have a plan, talk to your spouse about it before taking any action, and make sure the sale is a joint decision.

In another example, the company had two owners, one of whom brought in 50% of the sales and did project management. The other ran the operations, mainly squirreled away in his office. The former worked long hours and was indispensable. The latter didn't work as hard and was much easier to replace.

They put the business on the market and found a buyer they really liked, and it went downhill. They both wanted to keep their high paying jobs ($400,000 per year combined, which was a fair market salary for the person bringing in the business but not the admin owner) and also be paid for the business. This left little room for the buyer, who didn't want the admin owner around. This is not a workable situation. When it's time to get out, get out.

Having a post-sale plan will reduce stress and seller remorse, ease your buyer's fears, and make life a lot more enjoyable.

Chapter 10

Build a Team and Use Your Advisors

When I entered the buy-sell advisory business in the 1990s, my friend and mentor, Ted Leverette, emphasized to his clients that they can't be a "lone wolf" but needed to assemble a team of experts. Whether then, decades before, or now, it's important to have a team, and its members are about the same for both buyers and sellers.

The obvious first choice is a buy-sell expert (given I am one). I'll be the first to admit that a lot of deals are done without an intermediary on one or both sides. One of my great clients has bought four businesses. I helped him buy the first two, and he purchased the last two on his own. Another client has bought and sold numerous businesses, and he hired an associate and me to sell his last company. There's a lot of value in a good advisor, financial and emotional, so evaluate the risk-reward ratio.

Then comes a transaction attorney. Not your sister-in-law who's a family law attorney, not a bankruptcy attorney, not a personal injury attorney, and especially not a litigator (unless you want to negotiate forever and raise your bill sky-high), but an experienced transaction attorney for your size deal. For example, if your deal is $8 million, you don't want someone used to six-figure deals, and you don't want the middle market attorney used to $50-100 million deals. Your attorney needs the experience to know the standard middle legal ground, where deals get done.

Both sides need a tax accountant. The seller's accountant provides financial statements (hopefully reviewed so that sellers, as you prep for a sale, spend the money on a reviewed statement or two), and the buyer's accountant reviews the financial systems and statements, sets up the new system, etc. The accountants will collaborate on allocating the assets for tax purposes.

The buyer will also need a banker—and not just the manager of the branch where they make deposits. My three banker requirements are:

- The bank likes acquisition loans.

- The banker is experienced with acquisition loans.

- The bank can process loans when they say they will (early analysis) and on time.

Both sides—but especially the buyer—may need a human resources (HR) advisor, environmental consultant, CFO type, marketing firm, operations expert, or others, depending on the situation.

Now comes the critical part: *you must use your experts*. Don't be like the seller in Chapter 2 who suspended his attorney to save a few bucks, but it cost him more in aggravation than it was worth.

I have had clients who have used many of the specialty advisors mentioned above. Sellers have brought in people to improve operations (and margins), resolve HR issues and put them in compliance with HR laws, rules and regulations. Sellers have also hired CFOs to improve the management reports, set up budgets and valid cost accounting systems, and more. Buyers have used sellers' specialists plus marketing advisors to create a fresh look to get in front of more prospective customers.

So, again, create your team and use their expertise.

Chapter 11

Be an 'A' Business

In an issue of *Mergers & Acquisitions* magazine, a publication of the Association for Corporate Growth, an article mentioned sellers' and investment bankers' efforts to get "A" prices for "B" businesses.

Surprise, surprise! I don't think that's anything new. I don't think there are too many, if any, business owners who think they have anything but "A" businesses. It's just like how every football fan feels that the NFL draft gave their team the missing pieces to win the Super Bowl.

To me, any business making a profit after paying the owner a fair market salary for the work done is a "B" or better business. To get to the "A" level (which for a small business is different than if it's a middle-market business), a business must have the following usual suspects of a quality business:

- **A management team.** Which means the owner can take off for a month with no disruption. This is more than employees who just follow orders. This is having people who can make the right decisions, take charge, be independent, and yet be willing to accept delegation.

- **Consistent and growing profits, again, after paying the owner a fair market salary.** I laugh when I see things like, "The (high) price for this business is firm, given how solid the company is," when the business has lost money in two of the last three years. The numbers don't lie, unless someone manipulates them.

- **Sustainable growth with an understanding of why growth is occurring (quality of earnings).** Don't even think of saying,

"We could easily grow if we wanted to, I just don't want to." Show you can do it, have a plan, execute it, track the metrics, and you'll be able to demonstrate why growth can continue.

- **Achieving scale.** After all, it's rare that a business doing under $5 million in sales is a true "A" business. Keep in mind that a $15 million business with the same net profit margin as a $5 million business will get a higher multiple of earnings.

- **Solid financial systems and accurate financial statements.** Nothing frustrates a buyer more than having to figure out what the business is really making. The owner's sister-in-law who is really a data entry person but called a "controller" just won't cut it.

- **Be a leader in product quality, service and innovation.** You don't have as much value if your competitive advantage is the lowest price. Someone can always offer a lower price. Look at Grub Hub, Uber Eats, Door Dash and others. They lose money on every delivery as they attempt to gain market share by driving out competition.

- **Customer and vendor diversity, loyalty and strength.** There's another chapter on customer due diligence. Owners read it thoroughly and pay attention to it. The same goes for suppliers as it does for customers. You do not want one supplier, or you're handcuffed if that supplier has problems, is bought, raises prices, etc.

Buyers, this is for you also. You should want and be willing to pay "A" money for an "A" business. Don't fool yourself by thinking you can fix or improve every business you buy. There's a reason why "A" businesses sell for a premium compared to others. Don't pay "A" money for a "B" business. (Of course, buyers who pay "B" money for a "B" business because they know how to make it an "A" business will find they don't have as much buyer competition.)

"A" businesses will make more money, provide the owner more free time, and sell for more money. Be an "A" business.

What is Your Pay Grade?

Sellers: Is what you do on a daily, weekly, monthly basis commensurate with your pay grade? Buyers: Can you and do you want to do what the seller does?

Business owners should strive to cease doing things below their pay grade. Leverage yourself by having lower-compensated people do as much as they can. (There's a chapter on delegation; pay attention to it.)

What are some of the common things owners do below their pay grade? Here are some of them—and please realize I'm not saying owners shouldn't do these things at any time. My point is that the owner should strive to not be doing these things other than in a pinch or as a small part of their day (because they like doing this work once and a while).

- **Bookkeeping.** Enough said, bookkeepers are plentiful and inexpensive.

- **Making deliveries.** Unless it's to reinforce the relationship with an important customer.

- **HR.** There are plenty of experts available to handle the minutia and regulations.

- **Bidding or reviewing all bids.** The goal should be to have enough qualified people doing bids so that the owner is not needed to bid and trusts her people, and that the jobs are profitable.

- **Routine sales calls.** The owner's role should be to add value and let the customer know how important the relationship is, not to be "on the road."

- **Programming the machines.** Don't be like the business owner in Chapter 2 who refused to train his staff on how to program jobs because it would take an hour or two and he could do it 20 minutes while his people stood around waiting for him to finish.

- **Running the machines.** Some of the best owners don't know how to run their machines.

- **Designing products; being the only creative/artistic person.** It may be fun, it may be the owner's skill set, but it should evolve into becoming a design consultant, not the actual designer.

On the flipside, here are what owners should strive to do most of the time:

- **Strategy.** This means asking, "Where are we going, and how do we get there?"

- **Vision.** This means keeping an eye on the industry, customer issues, the economy, etc.

- **Enthusiasm.** One of the most important things an owner can do is to keep the employees happy, motivated, and productive.

- **Growth.** A flat or stable business is a stagnant business. An owner should always be focused on growth strategies.

- **Acquisitions.** A savvy owner will always be on the outlook for companies to bolt onto to gain new customers and employees, a new location, or any of the other 19 reasons to grow by acquisition, discussed in Chapter 61.

- **Process improvement.** One of the things I've noticed many buyers do is improve the processes, i.e. efficiencies in the operations. There is no reason why an owner can't get that done.

- **Managing the numbers (management reports, KPIs, etc.).** You don't have to be a CFO or controller to do so, but it's important to understand the key metrics for your business. It's more than the financial statements. Your CFO or controller (not a bookkeeper) should provide you with good management reports so you can see what's behind the numbers on the statements. Use them.

- **Leadership.** Many of the items above involve leadership. It's a lot different than management. Be a leader.

I realize the owner must do many of the tasks on the first list until the business grows to a scale where those tasks can be delegated. Yet, to receive a higher price and provide the buyer with maximum value and a better growth platform, an owner's objective should be to move toward doing the items on the second list.

Chapter 13

How Outdated is Your Technology?

I've come to the conclusion that even the least savvy business buyers realize there's a darn good chance the company's technology needs updating, and they'll put a cap ex line item into their budget for it. It's right up there with the accounting department when it comes to the category of, "Spend less, pay little attention to."

Business owners: Do yourself, your intermediary and your buyer a favor and stay up to date with your technology. Here are many of the questions buyers will ask you about, so realize that a pair of outside eyes (an IT managed service firm) is your best option to be confident about your technology.

- What are your cybersecurity programs?

- What techniques are in use to protect the integrity of networks, programs and data from attack, damage or unauthorized access?

- Disclose specific programs for security in-place.

- How do you handle breaches?

- Is cyber insurance in place or available?

A client's employee almost fell for phony email wire transfer scams. Friends of clients have wired money to bogus requests. We've all read about businesses and governments who've been blackmailed to unencrypt their systems (the city of Baltimore being one of the most prominent names). So know your computer systems, what you use them for, and who primarily does what on them.

- What software do you use?

- Are all of the copies of it legal and registered?

- Is any of it proprietary, and if so, do you own the license (or does the developer)?

Even after asking these questions, it was later determined that six copies of a design program were not licensed. Take the license fee per copy and factor in the multiplier for the deal, and you have a six-figure price reduction.

- How do you protect your IP?

- Are there trademarks or service marks?

- Is your email encrypted?

- Who develops and maintains your website?

- What are the costs of the development and maintenance, and how do you feel about the service?

- Are all pictures on your website owned or licensed?

- Who does your web hosting?

- What kind of web-hosting agreement do you have?

- When do your domain names expire?

- Who handles their renewal)?

Make sure you own your URLs. During one due diligence we found out that the tech service company owned the business' URL.

- What type of Internet access do your employees have when working offsite?

- Is the Internet access a VPN?

- Have you had any virus, malware, or spyware issues?

- Do you have anti-virus software?

- What are the dates of equipment purchases?

- What OS are you using?

It wasn't that long ago a buyer realized that the company was using five different versions of Windows, two of which were no longer Microsoft-supported. It was a patchwork mess the owner kept running, and some machines were over 15 years old. Scary, isn't it?

Final advice: This is just a start. I recommend hiring a managed services company to inspect and maintain all of your technology. It will save you in the long run.

Chapter 14

Don't be a C Corporation

We're talking small-to-mid-sized businesses here. One of my good CPA friends tells me that every year he tells clients to switch from C to S corporation status, but they don't do it, and when it comes time to sell, it's a (potentially costly) hassle. There are very few reasons why small businesses should remain C corporations. Remember, C corporations pay taxes on earnings, whereas S corporations are pass-through entities, and their owners show the earnings on their personal income tax returns.

Here's the dilemma. An "asset" sale of a C corporation, followed by the distribution of money to the owner(s), doubles the taxation. The corporation pays tax on the gain, and the owner(s) pay tax on the proceeds. So, the seller of a C corporation wants to do a stock sale so it's all capital gains tax rates.

But the buyer worries about inheriting all of the company history with a stock sale. Yes, the attorneys can protect the buyer from most things. But any lawsuit, or similar, is still a time-consuming hassle A lawsuit following a stock sale for actions prior to the sale will have the buyer included as part of the lawsuit and deeply involved in it, even if it's the seller's problem and obligation.

And then there's the financial loss to the buyer. At the time of writing this, the buyer is able to depreciate the assets on a new depreciation schedule and to amortize the goodwill over 15 years. (Let's hope there's a lot of goodwill, because that means a lot of profit.) This is often called "the C-corp trap," because the seller doesn't want to discount the price and the buyer doesn't want to lose the write-offs.

There are exceptions. One of the few cases where a stock sale made sense was for the sale of a company providing temporary housing for corporate new hires, people brought in for one to three months of training (e.g., airline mechanics coming to Boeing) and similar. With over 300 apartment leases, a stock sale was a no-brainer compared to assigning each lease or replacing it with a new one.

To complicate matters further, some owners own the real estate within the corporation (against their attorney's advice). If they sell the business to an outside buyer via a stock sale and the buyer doesn't want the real estate, they have to sell it to themselves (another entity), and the gain it creates has the same double-tax situation.

There is one possible solution if the deal is small enough for the buyer to "prove" he or she is absolutely integral to the success of the company: a dual sale with one sale to the buyer up to the company's basis and a sale of personal goodwill from the owner to the buyer. This gives the seller capital gains tax rates, and the buyer can write off the goodwill.

But this works only if the company is small enough. It may be hard to justify a lot of personal goodwill if the price is larger than $3-4 million. On one deal in this range, the buyer's CPA grilled the seller on what he did for the company, even though most of the onus is on the seller, as the CPA wanted to justify it. This won't work if a sizable management team is in place, if the owner isn't full time, etc.

The bottom line for most owners is: Don't be a C-corporation. If you are, convert to S-corporation status at least five years before selling. And before you do anything, check with your CPA and attorney.

Chapter 15

Owners, Know and Comply with All the HR Rules

Let's face it—we live in a very regulated point in time, especially when it comes to businesses, and double-especially when it comes to employees. I'm in Washington, one of the most employee-friendly states in the country, just behind California. Some states are more employer-friendly, and yet those owners still have to make sure they're complying with the myriad of laws, rules and regulations.

We all know HR is boring. It's overhead, and it can be a nuisance. Let's look at a list of items an owner needs to do correctly, and a buyer needs to research during due diligence.

Documentation. Do you have valid I-9 and W-4 forms for all employees? Buyers will, or at least ought to, check on this, and if it's an asset sale, they will be (re)hiring the employees and requiring new forms. An attorney recently told me about a deal in which the employee records were messy and incomplete. It took multiple employment attorneys over a week, onsite, to get them in order. Not inexpensive.

Vacation, PTO, etc. In the state of Washington we have vacation, PTO, sick pay, family leave, and more. Make sure you're not only doing it correctly but also have realistic policies. One owner had a very generous vacation policy plus 100% rollover. When it came time to sell, he paid out well over $100,000 prior to closing. The buyer hired an HR professional, updated all employee policies and procedures, and put in a "use it or lose it" vacation policy.

Harassment. Provide the proper training, monitor, and don't put up with even mild harassment of anybody. This can be as mild as risqué posters. Buyers may walk away if you sense a culture like this. And don't forget, this stuff can open you up to legal action.

Independent contractors. This is a hot-button issue for the IRS and State Departments of Revenue. The states want unemployment and L&I money, and the IRS knows many contractors don't report all their income. It sounds good to not pay the payroll taxes, but if caught, it's not worth it. I remember a company that cleaned medical facilities. They had all their people as contractors, had already been fined for it, refused to change, and couldn't sell their business because at current contract rates the cost of payroll burden ate up over half the profits.

Is it in writing? Have as much as you can in writing. Buyers, ask to *see* everything regarding HR; don't just take an owner's word on it. This means a policies-and-procedures manual, an employee handbook, job descriptions, training programs, hiring procedures, and more. Put all performance reviews, disciplinary notices, applications and resumes, incident tracking (even if you didn't discipline the behavior), etc., in writing.

Non-compete agreements. These vary state by state. In the state of Washington, a company can't have a non-compete agreement for an employee making under $100,000 ($250,000 if an independent contractor). But you can have a non-solicitation agreement so people can't leave and then recruit your customers or employees. Non-compete agreements are valid and enforceable on business sellers, because they're being compensated for it.

In summary, be cautious and detailed, and follow the rules. Buyers, make sure the business is in compliance. If unsure, hire an HR outsourcing firm or an employment attorney.

Chapter 16

Know What You're Selling

The best way to find out what a buyer will see is to put your company through a "mock" due diligence. A mock due diligence and a buyer's due diligence are very similar. Don't do it yourself. Hire an outside pair of eyes to do it, as it is human nature to miss things we are closest to.

Your job is to anticipate what a buyer will ask and to ready the business for investigation. Know the different buyer types and their objectives. As with many things in life, Pareto's Principle holds true here (also known as the 80-20 rule): buyers of all types and sizes will be concerned with the same 80 percent of issues in an acquisition target.

Most potential buyers will not be very interested in doing much legal due diligence, because they will not want to buy your stock. Keep in mind that you will represent and warranty that everything you provide the buyer is true and correct, so have a good understanding of the details. The reps and warranties also come with indemnification if you misrepresented anything.

The first area most buyers go to is financial due diligence. In today's world, accountants typically look backward as they prepare financial statements and tax returns. CFOs and other finance people look forward and help with budgets, systems, and management reporting. Both are important, as is telling them your objective, so that everybody is working toward the same goal.

And remember: the larger your firm and the more complicated your business, the more scrutiny you will receive. A buyer off by 10 percent on a $1 million deal and a buyer who is off by 10 percent on a $10 million deal both have issues, just different ones. And if the debt coverage ratio is too low to start, any hiccup can hurt cash flow and cause the bank to react with stringent oversight. Here are the top seven financial due diligence areas, as financial experts have shared with me:

1. Financial Statements

2. Financial Systems

3. Management Reports

4. Banks and Your Banker

5. Balance Sheet

6. Profits (as in, what is the true free cash flow)

7. Statement of cash flows

If you're sizable enough, consider having your financial statements "reviewed," which means the CPA reviews your statements to ensure that they are done according to accounting standards and they summarize company issues, but they take what you say as true and correct (no auditing, inventory-counting, etc.). This adds a lot of credibility and makes the quality of earnings report a lot easier.

Smart buyers will concentrate on the non-financial factors, including customers, employees, management, suppliers, the market, competition, etc. Consider having a third party talk to your customers, as a reference check. Have an outside party "interview" your key employees, asking the same questions a buyer will ask. And the same for all other factors. This allows you to update any weaknesses before a buyer uncovers them.

Don't Do What Your Employees Can Do

What this title means is, *delegate*. You must eliminate the most critical dependency a firm can have, and that is when everything—or a majority of important things—depend on the owner's involvement. I've seen companies with over 50 employees in which the owner was the key cog in the operations, and I remember one company with 12 employees where we determined it was really an 11-person operation because the owner did almost nothing.

Delegating is not always easy, especially to a founder who knows the product or operations as well as anybody in the industry. Delegating entails letting go. Before that, it takes hiring the right people. Believe me, a buyer would prefer to hear that you have great employees with a salary range at the high end than that you have mediocre employees at the low end of the salary range.

I was taught that delegating has three components:

1. **You (and your management team) must be willing to delegate.** This is often the toughest element. It can be hard to let go, to let people stumble and bruise themselves (and maybe hurt the company a little). But if you don't let them stumble and learn on small things, what happens when they are forced to deal with big issues?

2. **Your employees at all levels must be willing to accept delegation.** Some people just don't want responsibility, and they are easy to sort out. It's the people who *do* want to grow, advance and contribute that you want to nurture

and train. They will rise to the top, volunteer to take on projects, and be willing to learn.

3. **There must be a culture where delegation is acceptable.** Pick up any business publication, and chances are you will find an article on the workplace, bad managers, good managers, or similar. You may be willing to delegate, employees may be willing to accept delegation, and others may not accept it and may actually sabotage it. Perhaps they are jealous that they weren't delegated to or promoted. In any event, if you can make delegation acceptable, it will impress your buyers, who will all want to grow the business and use your team to do so.

Here are the wrong way and the right way to delegate:

- Behind his back, employees referred to Steve's "drive-bys." He had a habit of hovering over an employee's desk or cubicle, fidgeting for a minute or two, then blurting out something like, "Don't worry about that, it's just my money!" and stomping off. Nice culture of appreciation, isn't it?

- Tom did things differently. As a sales guy, he knew he had to let his management team handle the operations, production, and administration in his 80-strong company. His six-person management team worked well together, they knew their roles, and their employees loved them. I know this firsthand, because after I worked with this firm I had them do some work for me. What a difference when the employees at all levels are empowered and respected!

 **18**

Is the Buyer Who They Say They Are?

The vast majority of business owners/sellers use their gut to tell them if it's the right buyer. An intermediary will do some due diligence on the buyer, and all too often it's nothing more than asking for a resume and a personal financial statement.

That said, the relationship is the top element of diligence on the buyer. Almost no sellers want to sell to someone who won't keep the employees hired, preserve the name and legacy, and, above all, won't be able to pay the seller note. You have to like and trust the buyer, as well as respect that person's business acumen.

Sellers should approach buyer meetings as if they were friendly job interviews. You want to know what makes the person tick, what they've done, and how they've done it. To that end you should ask the following questions, as a minimum:

1. Why do you want to own a business?
2. What plans do you have for managing my business?
3. Tell me about yourself.
4. What makes you think you are qualified to buy my business?
5. How does your experience relate to my business?
6. Why are you leaving your job? (Or why don't you have a job?)
7. Why do you want another company?
8. Why did it take so long for you to decide to become self-employed?
9. What failures have you experienced?
10. Who are a few references who can attest to your capabilities and integrity?

The last question is interesting in that I can't ever remember a seller asking a buyer for references, even though the buyer will want to talk to the company's customers, employees and vendors.

Note: A good buyer should ask great questions about the business, its potential, you, what the owner does, what you've tried (whether it worked or didn't), your employees, etc. On the flipside, a buyer moving too fast may be snooping, not a serious buyer, naïve, or so full of themselves they won't seek professional advice and have a higher probability of failing.

Also realize that, if there's a bank involved, the bank will screen the buyer based on financial capabilities, skills, personality, and seriousness. After all, good bankers don't want to waste time on tire-kickers.

What makes a buyer qualified? In simple terms, this three-legged stool says it all.

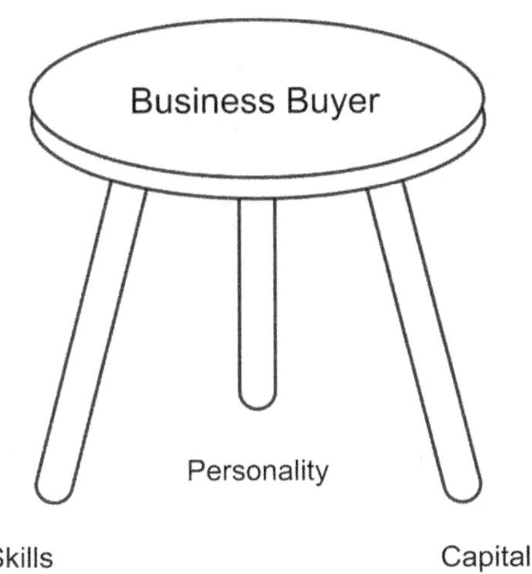

Buyers, Know the Banking Rules; Sellers, Know the Banking Rules

The banks have the money; the banks make the rules. The Golden Rule, right? Both buyer and seller need to know the basics of lending programs, rules, and process. This starts with realizing whether the loan qualifies for the Small Business Administration (SBA) loan guarantee program (guaranteed to the bank by the SBA). The bank will almost always use this program, if they can, as they get at least 75% of the loan guaranteed.

First let's cover non-SBA loans. These are for deals with investment groups whose members won't sign the required SBA personal guarantee and/or are larger than the SBA limits. (As I write this, the ceiling is now a loan of $5 million including fees.) For deals over the SBA limit, the bank will probably lend about three times earnings. This is considered senior debt, meaning first in line to get repaid. The term will probably be five years, and sometimes seven. The buyer will have to put down 25% of the price, and these loans are more focused on collateral.

SBA loans are different animals. Basic facts about them include:

- The SBA guarantees most of the loan to the bank, and the buyers pays for it via a ~3% loan fee, which is basically an insurance policy.

- Each loan has a 10-year amortization, which is gentle on cash flow.

- The borrower (anybody with 20% or more ownership) will sign a personal guarantee.

- A minimum of buyer cash equal to (only) 10% of total project costs.

- The banks underwrite it to their standards, so different banks may make different offers.

- The banks will be nosy.

- These are cash-flow loans, meaning the bank doesn't need full collateral. They will take business collateral and home/real estate equity. And the more collateral, the lower the interest rate, generally.

No matter what lending program you use, the banks will look at the debt coverage ratio based on historical earnings (after allowing for a fair market owner's salary). Most banks' minimum ratio is 1.25:1, and good bankers won't want it below 1.5:1. Small deals, under about $2 million, should have a 2:1 ratio to protect both buyer and seller from cash-flow issues. In simple terms, this means, for every dollar of debt payment, principal and interest, the company should have either $1.50-$2.00 of pre-tax earnings.

We go through waves of bank underwriting policies. They were very loose in the mid-2000s, then they became very tight (as they should be). After the Great Recession, banks got back to the more thorough underwriting and paying attention to the five C's of banking:

- **Capacity**—How will you repay the money? There had better be cash flow to support your debt payments, or why would anybody lend you the money? Without capacity, you'll be dependent on the next factor.

- **Collateral**—What does the lender get if you can't make the payments? Believe me, the bank does not want your truck, house, car, equipment, or anything else. The bank wants to be repaid, thus it severely discounts the value of the assets used as collateral.

- **Capital**—This is your skin in the game—also known as your risk. As in the story below, your capital (as an owner, buyer, or seller) is more important than it was in recent years.

- **Conditions**—What is the loan for? Banks usually want to tie long-term needs (a piece of equipment or a business acquisition) to a term loan. Short-term needs (working capital) will be tied to a line-of-credit loan, like an accounts receivable line of credit that will be paid back when your customer pays you.

- **Character**—Like you selling your product, or selling your business, it's a relationship game with your banker. You must come across as competent, trustworthy, experienced, and of solid reputation.

Buyers, here's something from a bank president on buyer's collateral and use of home equity as collateral: "If you aren't confident enough in your business and its prospects to mortgage your house and put your life savings into it, then why should I have confidence in you?"

I Want to Make an Offer; I Want to Get an Offer

This is what it's all about: making and getting an offer, a fair offer that will lead to closing the deal. Sounds easy—"Make an offer!"—but it's really pretty complicated. Let's look at the big-picture steps.

As mentioned elsewhere, it starts with having a solid relationship. No relationship, no trust, no confidence in the other party means no offer, therefore no deal.

The next step is analysis. For that, the buyer must get financial information, at least three years of financial statements (profit-and-loss statement, balance sheet, and hopefully a statement of cash flows), and monthly year-to-date statements (really important in the COVID-19 era). The buyer should also uncover any red flags (more on this below). Simultaneously, the seller should review the buyer's background and financial capabilities and then assess whether the buyer appears qualified.

Using this information, the buyer makes an offer. Let's cut to the chase: buyers rarely make their best offers first, just as the asking price is rarely the minimum the seller will take. The offer should include price, terms, and conditions.

There's usually a bit of back-and-forth, followed by a signed non-binding letter of intent.

Then the fun begins—due diligence. There's more on this in other chapters, and due diligence essentially confirms what the seller has told the buyer, and vice versa. For example, during analysis, the buyer will get a list of sales by revenue or percentage of revenue, but without the customer names. During diligence, he gets the names.

If all is confirmed (no surprises, just confirmation), the deal should close.

I mentioned above about uncovering red flags. The best way to do that is with our "Initial Disclosure Form"; if you'd like a copy, email john@johnmartinka.com. It's a request for basic information with over 30 yes-or-no questions to uncover areas to investigate before making an offer. Here are seven of those questions:

1. Are there any revenue or expense items which relate to your business that do not appear on its financial statements?

2. Has the company had an IRS or State Department of Revenue audits in the last seven years, and/or have there been any tax liens, reprimands, fines or similar?

3. Is there any past, current and/or pending/anticipated litigation in which the firm is involved?

4. Does any customer represent more than 10% of your business' annual gross revenue?

5. Do you have any people working as independent contractors who could possibly be considered employees?

6. Do you have any off-balance sheet assets or liabilities (leases, long-term service contracts, yellow page [or other] advertising contracts, etc.)?

7. What are the estimated capital expenditures the next few years?

A seller should want to disclose any "warts" as soon as possible. No business is perfect, and buyers know this. What buyers want is opportunity. When they see where they can add value, they'll want the business. Little red flags won't get in the way. Big red flags, or finding out something the seller tried to not disclose, will kill or hurt the deal.

Advisory Boards are a Bad Idea if You Answer Yes to These Three Questions

By John O'Dore, Co-founder, Chinook Capital Advisors

Question #1: Are you fully prepared for the rigor of third-party financial, operational, and legal due diligence covering at least the last three (3) years of business?

Yes or No?

Question #2: Do you fully understand all of the value-drivers in your business from a buyer's perspective? Have you proactively taken corrective action to address red- and yellow-flag issues in advance that would prevent your business from achieving a maximum value?

Yes or No?

Question #3: Do you fully understand all of the tax implications in the sale of your business, as well as the differences between a stock sale and an asset sale? Have you taken proactive steps to minimize taxes and maximize net proceeds in a sale?

Yes or No?

If you answered "yes" to all three questions, you are in the minority of business owners we speak with. Most are too busy running their companies to focus on these issues, or by nature they tend to procrastinate until something becomes urgent.

What is an advisory board? It is a select group of professional advisors hand-picked by a business owner to help prepare the company for a transition of ownership. In our experience, the focus should be to:

1.　maximize the net proceeds from the sale, and

2.　increase the probability that a transaction closes.

Who typically is on an advisory board? An advisory board should generally include an M&A advisor, a corporate attorney with expertise in company sale transactions, and a CPA. Other advisors to include, depending on the situation, could be a personal financial planner or wealth advisor, a trust attorney, or other consultants with expertise in specific areas such as executive compensation or finance.

What does an advisory board do? An advisory board helps a business owner identify and resolve specific issues that would reduce the likelihood of their company receiving a premium valuation in a sale. The board works as directed by the business owner and has no decision-making authority.

Advisory boards can meet monthly, bimonthly, quarterly, or even semi-annually, depending on the situation. Typically, the business owner sets up an action plan or set of "to dos" to accomplish before the next meeting with the board. Failing to address these issues with the board could potentially reduce a company's valuation by millions of dollars if they are unresolved prior to a sale transaction.

Summary: Selling a business is complex, and since it has no "do-overs," it is worth the extra effort, time, and money to be properly prepared. The result could be millions of dollars in increased value and peace of mind throughout the process.

John O'Dore
Chinook Capital Advisors
John@chinookadvisors.com

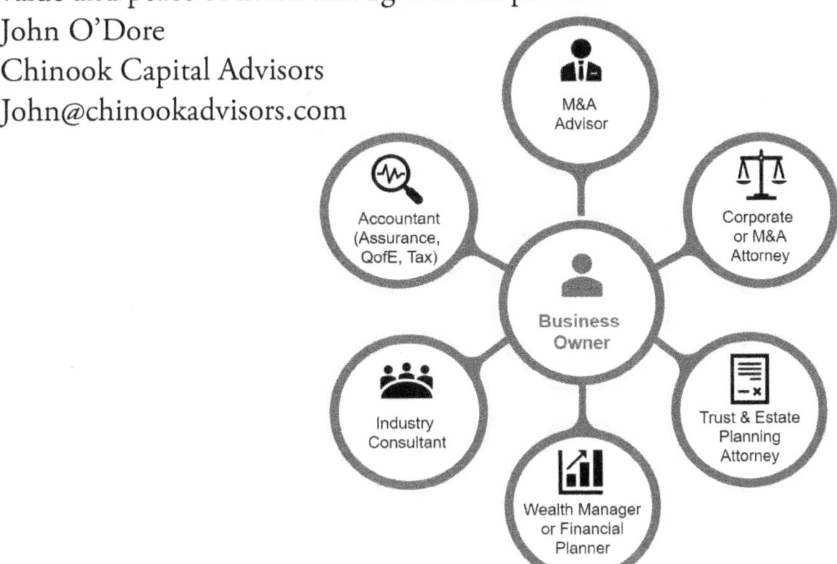

Chapter 22

Get the Players on the Same Field...Early

By Pete McDowell, Business Advisor, RC Advisory Services

There are always challenges in getting a deal done when dealing with a seller and buyer. Often it's a matter of miscommunication or lack of knowledge about the process of selling a business. Here are ten things we've learned to ensure a smooth process and a mutually satisfying close:

1. Letter of Intent from the buyer. When there is seller financing as a part of the deal (in addition to Bank Financing) make sure a clause is in the LOI along these lines: buyer will provide a Personal Financial Statement for evaluation by the seller, and buyer will sign a Personal Guarantee for the seller note.

2. Establish deal teams for both seller and buyer within two weeks after the Letter of Intent. These teams must include the CPA and law firms, bankers, seller's commercial insurance agency, and financial planners. Everyone needs to be on the same page of the initial deal structure and its ramifications. The sooner the better.

3. Encourage both seller and buyer to authorize their respective legal and accounting teams to communicate directly, to efficiently and effectively drive the process. Clarify up front what expectations are for overall fees, to keep costs in check.

4. Both parties ***must use*** law and CPA firms with sufficient staff. That way, the parties can be responsive to the normal and quick changes that occur during the final stages of the transaction process. Use a firm with at least four professionals, in addition to administrative staff. It gets hectic and intense, and having

the firepower available to manage all details in an expedient manner is critical.

5. Involve the CPAs immediately in calculating expected proceeds, including the tax plan.

6. Identify the closing attorney and funds transfer function very early on. This lets everyone know what the expectation is around how much money will change hands and where it will be disbursed. It may change slightly as professional fees are adjusted or working capital changes over the course of the due diligence and PSA timeframe.

7. Confirm phone calls and sidebar conversations with follow-up recap emails to avoid what is called 'convenient memory.' Because of the emotional component of selling a business and the numerous changes in the transaction details over the final weeks, people forget key agreements they were a party to. When this happens, it throws a 'wrench in the gears' of the transaction motor and can lead to feelings of distrust and angst.

8. Remind prospective clients that due diligence typically results in the buyer finding 'things' that can indicate higher risk to the buyer than anticipated. These findings, many of which the seller is not aware of, will lead to downward pressure on the price.

9. Don't overanalyze the financials, as complex models may lead the buyer to erroneous conclusions. Keep the model as macro as possible with just enough detail to support bank-financing applications.

10. The buyer should develop his/her own Pro-Forma, which takes into account extraordinary costs or revenue opportunities discussed during due diligence. It is the buyer's responsibility to develop the Pro-Forma, one that includes debt servicing.

Pete McDowell
RC Advisory Services
pmcdowell@rcadvisorysvcs.com
425-577-3503

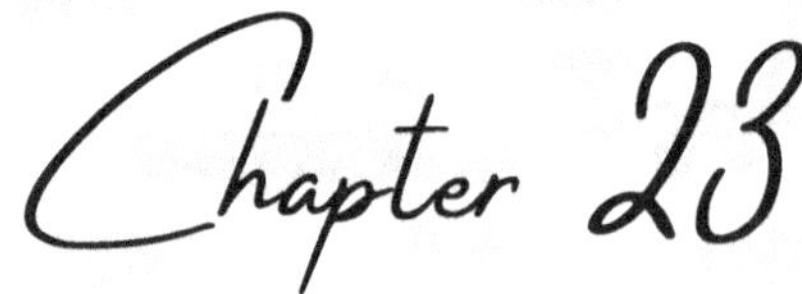

20 Rules of Business Buying

1. **Searching for a business is sales.** It is the same as a business prospecting for customers. Devise a proven search plan, and execute it properly.

2. **Cash is king.** And so is cash flow.

3. **The queen is relationships, and, as in chess, the queen is the most powerful piece in the game.** It's a relationship game, and don't forget it; nobody buys from or sells to someone they don't like.

4. **You won't "know it when you see it."** You must define your criteria.

5. **Correspondingly (to the previous rule), when you see where you can add real value, you will get excited and want to take action to buy that particular company.**

6. Show confidence, speed and creativity.

7. **Growth hides a lot of operational warts.** And those warts tend to work their way out.

8. **Don't fall in love with the product.** Fall in love with the business model and its value proposition. This means you want a business with a defensible competitive advantage.

9. **The bigger the spreadsheet, the less chance of a deal.** Don't get analysis-paralysis.

10. There are no perfect businesses and no perfect deals.

11. What makes you a good business owner can make you a bad deal person.

12. Terms are often more important than price.

13. **Watch out for dependencies in the business.** The first place to look is at the owner. How dependent is the business on the owner?

14. **Due diligence is for proving what you've been told, and on what you based your offer.** It is not time for surprises.

15. **Educate the seller on the process.** Make sure the seller understands the bank. Be "nosy."

16. You can't be a "defensive" buyer.

17. The administrivia near closing will drive you nuts, but it must be done.

18. **Make your starting benchmark for financing 50% of profit to acquisition debt.** This will involve a 2:1 debt coverage ratio.

19. **You will make a leap of faith.** Do it right, and that leap will be off a chair, not the roof.

20. **The only thing worse than no deal is a bad deal.** Be patient, and don't get "buyer fever."

Finding a Business is Like Finding a Job—It Takes Work

This strategy is primarily for buyers, but sellers need to pay attention to it as well. My friend and career coach, Matt Youngquist with Career Horizons (www.career-horizons.com), published a newsletter with the following statements.

1. Less than 20% of all hiring that takes place in today's market occurs from submitting a resume or application to a published Internet opportunity.

2. Such listings are often the most rigid, competitive method for being hired.

3. The most successful job hunters realize that the main avenue for success has always been the networking circuit, and they channel the majority of their efforts each day into building relationships, identifying target companies, and seeking to generate referrals into these organizations.

4. This really isn't new information, as virtually every career book and article has cited these realities for the past decade or two, but for whatever reason there seems to have been a "relapse" of people lately who are putting too much faith—and investing too much time—on the job website circuit

5. Most hiring activity out there never actually sees the light of the day and is generated through "warm" interpersonal interactions, instead of through the chilly, unfeeling clutches of resume-screening software.

Matt could have been writing for me with a few edits. So let's look at those edits to make his points relevant to those interested in business buy-sell.

1. The International Business Brokers Association and other sources have stated for years similar statistics for the sales of small businesses. They state 20% or so of profitable companies sold are advertised or listed, although my impression is that, the larger the company, the greater the chance an intermediary will be involved. Business buyers and sellers must access 100% of the market.

2. Using email and the Internet can be the "easy way out"—and this applies to buyers and sellers. It's a lot easier to screen someone out if relying on only a resume or application.

3. A focal point in my book, *Buying A Business That Makes You Rich*, is that buyers must get out and "pound the pavement." They must make calls, meet people, and build relationships. People sell to and refer to people they like.

4. So why won't/don't most business buyers do this? We know why sellers don't do it: confidentiality, lack of knowledge of what to do (and how to do it confidentially), and having been cold-called too many times by rookie brokers.

5. There is no screening software for business buy-sell deals (yet) so refer to my first point. Many deals are done directly from seller to buyer. As mentioned, sellers fear (and this is a mild word) a confidentiality breach, and some prefer to work one-on-one with a qualified buyer. (Of course, many prefer to see as many buyers as possible and don't really worry that buyers can figure the name of their company based on the Internet ad.)

Buyers and sellers need to figure out who their logical targets are and do whatever they can to stealthily get in front of those targets.

What are the Three Key Factors in Getting the Deal Done?

Rarely do audiences understand even one of the top three factors to getting a deal done. Most of their answers are things like price, cash, terms, or similar. While these are important, you don't get to them unless there is:

- Motivation

- Relationship

- Education

If the seller's *motivation* is to get grossly overpaid, there will be no deal. If the buyer's motivation is to get a "bottom-feeder" type deal, there will be no deal (on a good business). For sellers, the motivation needs to be things like retirement, health, (extreme) burnout, the business has outgrown the owner, etc. The more catastrophic the event (divorce, death, disability, etc.), the greater the urgency.

For an individual buyer, it's because he lost his job, fears losing it, or has used the corporate world to build skills and grow capital, always having known he wanted to own a business but not being the startup type.

For a company, it can be any of the 19 reasons why a business should consider growth by acquisition (as described in the chapter from my book *Company Growth By Acquisition Makes Dollars & Sense* at the end of this book). The most common reasons are: to be a larger firm, to get good employees, to diversify customer and/or product base, and to expand geographically.

Once we have a motivated buyer and seller, there has to be a great *relationship* between them. As a client who had sold one and bought two companies said to me, "I would never buy from or sell to somebody I don't like." This means the initial meeting between parties is more about finding commonality, establishing rapport, and building a relationship. Details of the business can wait.

In the small, mid-sized and lower middle-markets, the buyer and seller must have a bond, or there is almost no chance of a deal.

Then comes *education* in how the process works and what to expect. First, nobody should expect total smooth sailing. There will be stops and starts. One intermediary I know says all deals die at least once—or at least they smack into a roadblock and need recovery. Your education should include awareness of the following roadblocks to expect:

- *You will get frustrated.* You'll get frustrated over the pace (too slow), the never-ending questions (just when the seller thinks they've answered every possible question, the bank asks more), the lawyers, and because the CPA is off doing taxes right when you need her.

- *Different-sized business have given ranges of value, backed up by incredible amounts of data.* It's rare that the selling price is outside of these ranges (more on this in other chapters). So, Mr. Seller, your business isn't so special that it will sell for more. And Ms. Buyer, you aren't going to pay the value of the assets just because you don't think you should pay for blue sky. Connected to this point are two other factors:

- *There is (usually) a difference between what financial buyers like individuals will pay and what strategic buyers like a company in the same industry, a supplier, or even a customer will pay.* If strategic buyers believe they can create synergies and reduce expenses, they will (usually) pay more than otherwise.

- *Current market conditions can apply.* Things were different during the Great Recession. Things are different as I write this during COVID-19. Currently, businesses that have done well during the virus and the related shutdown are selling for the same multiple of earnings as before, or even higher. Those that were hurt sell for less, if they sell at all.

In sum, both parties must be *motivated* for the right reasons, there has to be a trusting *relationship*, and a lot of *education* is necessary to reduce frustration and "deal fatigue."

Chapter 26

Business Buy-Sell is a Contact Sport, so Make a Lot of Contacts

By Jessica Martinka, Martinka Consulting

Business buyers and sellers pay attention. The key to finding a great match to buy from or sell to is to get in front of as many qualified people as possible, confidentially if you're a seller. Think of it as *building relationships.*

Buyers: The more people who know you are looking for a business, the better. You never know when someone will hear of a seller and think of you.

- *Tell everyone you know that you are searching for a business to buy.* Whether they are from business, family, clubs/groups, etc., ask them if they know of anyone who is thinking of selling their business. You might not get a lead right away, but you have nothing to lose spreading the word to as many people as you can.

- *Stay in touch with them.* If they hear from you only once, they'll figure you found something or gave up your search.

- *Don't rely solely on your network!* Get in touch with brokers, and follow up on a consistent basis so they know you are a serious buyer who is ready to make a move on the right opportunity. You want them to call you first when a new listing appears.

Sellers: You can't do the above. *Stealth* is your strategy, because you don't want employees, customers, suppliers, or competitors to know you're selling a business.

- *Start with your attorney, CPA, banker, and others you know can keep your goal confidential.* To really spread the word—confidentially—use a broker or investment banker. Tip: If they can market your business without advertising it, so much the better.

- *When hiring an intermediary, don't hire the first one you meet.* Consider interviewing multiple intermediaries. Make sure you get along with, and trust, that person. Find out how that individual will market your business without revealing your identity. Sellers often want their intermediaries to work their networks and databases before advertising the business.

Whether you're a buyer or seller, realize that networking is not just about asking and receiving. "Give to get" should be your mantra. When I offer value to people in my network, it feels more like helping a friend than selling our services.

When meeting with people, remember: *it's all about relationships.* As stated elsewhere in this book, one of our past clients said, "I would never buy a business from or sell to someone I didn't like." It is a true statement.

Networking will uncover businesses on the hidden market for buyers; these are often do-it-yourself sellers. You will only get introduced to them if people know you're searching. For sellers, networking can introduce you to those buyers you might not otherwise find.

Having trustworthy advisors on your team is just as important. As a seller, your banker, CPA, and attorney can help by confidentially asking their network if they have any potential buyers for you to meet.

Cast a wide net—you can never have enough opportunities!

Jessica Martinka
Martinka Consulting
Jessica@martinkaconsulting.com
425-391-6984

Chapter 27

The Top Five Things to Know About Business Opportunity Syndications

By Greg Russell, Lawyer, PRK Livengood PLLC

Our clients interested in purchasing an operating business often look to use money from investors to provide the capital needed to acquire these businesses and to bridge the gap between the acquisition cost and the financing provided by the bank and the seller of the business. These clients thus get involved, intentionally or not, in a business securities syndication. If a person uses money from investors to acquire a business, then that person must be careful to comply with the detailed and complex rules around properly structuring a business syndication. Here is a top-five list of legal issues to consider in a syndication.

1. **Is the Project a Securities Offering or Syndication?** In a syndication, a "sponsor" or "syndicator" individual or entity identifies a business they want to buy, hold and/or grow, and then sell for a profit. The sponsor looks to investors to provide some or all of the equity capital needed to accomplish this, and shares the profits with those investors in some manner. Thus any person or entity that takes money from investors who are relying on the sponsor's expertise to make the business a success is engaged in a securities offering or syndication, which means they need to comply with all relevant securities laws associated with a syndication.

2. **Are the Investors Accredited?** A key rule around syndications is that the sponsor needs to qualify for an exemption from reg-

istering the equity interests (called "securities") being sold to investors as a public offering. The most common exemption syndicators use is taking capital only from accredited investors. There are specific guidelines for who is considered an accredited investor and how you qualify someone as one. Other exemptions are available to sell equity to non-accredited investors, but these are generally more difficult and costly to meet. Failure to follow these rules strictly can invalidate your exemption and expose the sponsor to personal liability to the investors if the business does not perform to expectations.

3. **Are Disclosures Comprehensive.** Another prime element in a properly structured syndication is the need to disclose to investors all information a "reasonably prudent" investor would want to know before making the investment. This includes disclosures about the business, as well as the legal, financing and business risks associated with the opportunity. Typically a sponsor will prepare a detailed set of written disclosures (sometimes called a private placement memorandum, or PPM) that is provided to investors. For smaller businesses, a subscription agreement with disclosures attached as an exhibit may be sufficient.

4. **Have All Federal and State Filings Been Done?** Before raising capital and accepting money from investors, a sponsor is required to make certain notice filings with the federal and state securities regulators to qualify their offering for the specific securities exemptions they are seeking. This step is often missed or forgotten by new syndicators and can again invalidate the securities offering and expose the sponsor to personal liability.

5. **How are Investors Solicited?** A primary rule around syndications focuses on how the sponsor finds investors. The traditional rule is that a sponsor cannot advertise or publicly solicit for investors. However, in recent years this rule has been relaxed

some, and now there are options to solicit investors through databases like LinkedIn or other social media, or through online platforms and similar avenues. However, the rules around this kind of public solicitation are complex, require additional disclosures to investors, and put additional responsibilities on the sponsor that require careful planning and documentation before embarking on this kind of solicitation.

Greg Russell
PRK Livengood
grussell@prklaw.com

Blue Sky vs. Bottom-feeder

This may sound like hyperbole, but I've heard the following statements from buyers and sellers.

- Seller: "Everything is for sale. If someone wants to pay me X dollars, I'm glad to sell [when X dollars is about four times the true value of the business]."

- Buyer: "My CPA says a business is worth its book value. So why would I pay more?"

- Seller: "My business is worth the value of the assets, the goodwill, and something for the growth potential."

- Buyer: "I'm looking for an elderly seller of a profitable business with no family members in the business. That seller doesn't have any other options, so he'll sell to me for a small down payment plus a note." (Actually, the seller of a profitable business with no family involved has all the options.)

There are generally accepted price ranges in which businesses sell. These are ranges, not absolutes, because two seemingly similar businesses may be very different under the hood. One may have customer concentration issues, while the other has a very diverse group of customers. One may have a solid management team, whereas the other may have the owner and nobody else.

Sellers: Please realize that, even though you saw in *The Wall Street Journal* that a $300 million business in your industry sold for 10X EBITDA, your business doing $3 million or $30 million will not sell for 10X. Also realize that most buyers won't pay for potential (yes, there are exceptions, but they're rare, and that's why they're exceptions). Buyers are interested in your business because they believe that it has potential and that such potential can be exploited by the value they bring to the company. But they pay based on the business history. (And banks lend based on the business history.)

Buyers: What do you want? A mediocre business at a great price, or a fantastic business at a fair price? Don't win the battle and lose the war. Pay a fair price, apply your skills, grow the business, and in a couple of years look back and ask, "Why was I worried about paying X (or 115% of X)?"

I got the above statement from a client. He actually said, "I don't care if I pay $X or $X plus 15%; I know what I can do with this business." That's the buyer a seller wants. That's the business a buyer wants. Pretty simple—or so it seems.

The vast majority of my clients' deals are not "screaming deals." Nor are they "overpriced deals." They are within the fair range, and a major determining factor of that is the relationship between buyer and seller. Most sellers want their customers taken care of, their employees secure and happy, and legacy. All buyers want a company they can scale. These two factors go hand-in-hand.

Price is important to both sides. But the right buyer for the right business is *the* most important factor. Don't let the good match get away. All the same, remember: there are no perfect businesses, perfect buyers, or perfect deals.

What's Scary: A Breach of Confidentiality

Jim was selling his business to a friendly competitor. He felt obligated to let his two key employees know what was going on, over my objections. Within a week, both gave notice, scared of the uncertainty. Luckily for him, he was able to convince one of them to return, or the deal may have collapsed.

I was speaking to a CPA group when one lady began bouncing up and down in her seat (I thought I had missed the break time) as I mentioned that an owner had told me he was put on COD (cash on delivery) when he told a vendor he was "thinking of selling" the business. She urgently wanted to let me know that her company did the same thing if they found out a distributor was selling, or even thinking of it.

I've seen numerous situations where customers started looking for alternate suppliers when they found out a business was for sale.

The above are why owners/sellers are scared to death about a breach of confidentiality. Which brings us to the use of non-disclosure agreements. NDAs are a necessary requirement for doing business, especially when the sale of a company is involved.

In reality, they are a formal show of good faith. If a buyer balks at signing one, wants it to be very loose, or objects to reasonable language, then something is wrong (probably with that buyer). On the flipside, if a seller's attorney has made it so restrictive (I've seen ones that prohibit the buyer from entering the industry for 3-5 years) then watch out—it won't be an easy path to doing a deal.

My advice is, if you don't trust the other party, an NDA won't do you much good. There's also an education factor. A good intermediary will remind buyers to take the NDA seriously. They're trying to avoid the buyer who thinks it doesn't matter if they talk to their friends, their dentist, golfing buddies, or anybody else about the business. Once they say the name of the business, it starts spreading. On that subject, what usually triggers the word "getting out" is the buyer's application for government licenses, permits, and similar. Inevitably, the government agency sends it to the business's address, even when instructed not to.

There are exceptions, but they're rare. Many years ago, we went to one of our favorite restaurants, and in the menu was a note saying, "We're retiring and want to sell. Do you know any buyers?" Occasionally an owner will, as part of the exit planning, bring employees, vendors, and even customers into the loop. (What's really rare is an owner who does actual exit planning.)

Realize that it goes both ways. Individual buyers may not want it out that they're looking to buy and leave their jobs. Small businesses may want to keep it quiet, so that their employees don't think they're going to be replaced or that competitors will make a run at the target company.

To summarize, it's not the language as much as the willingness (to sign). A simple confidentiality agreement stating, "I won't tell anybody other than my advisors and spouse" is as good as the long, legalese document (in my non-lawyer experience).

Chapter 30

Be Collaborative

Think of the following situations:

- Union negotiations are intense, and the parties often can't stand each other

- Pro sports are extremely competitive, and tempers often flare

- Apple vs. Samsung vs. Google vs. Microsoft

- Democrats vs. Republicans

But small-to-mid-sized business buy-sell can't be confrontational, or there won't be a deal. The buyer and seller have to live with each other for months, or even years. The buyer has to work with the management and other employees, and if they know the buyer and seller are fighting, guess whose side they'll take (usually not the buyer's)? Talk about a way to quickly destroy the culture!

Buy-sell deals must feature collaboration. The parties have to like each other, and the advisors have to work together to make sure things go smoothly. There is give-and-take, and not everybody will get what they wish and hope for (e.g., a super-high price all in cash, or a rock-bottom price with almost no down payment).

The deals that go fastest and smoothest are those where all the parties understand that a successful deal is the only goal that really matters. It doesn't help to win a bunch of little battles if you lose the war, which you may lose if you drive the other side crazy with nagging requests (always wanting a little more, etc.).

Example (on how not to do it): Don't be like the (almost) seller whose deal died after she insisted on controlling so many things, including insisting that the business would be run "as I ran it," and she had to review the buyer's employment agreements to make sure they were "exactly like mine." The buyer ran away, and fast.

So how do you collaborate? Here are three areas on which to concentrate.

1. *Do you have the best match possible?* If so, you need to make it happen. For sellers, this means: Is it the right buyer? Does your picture of the logical buyer fit your actual buyer? For buyers: Is this a business where you can add value? Can you see yourself going to work at this company every day (and contributing to it)? If yes, realize you need to get the deal done.

2. *Look at the relationship with the other party.* Is this someone with whom you would want to have a drink, go out for dinner, or take a cruise? It's not easy to find people you can relate with on many levels. If you've found one, get the deal done.

3. *Don't worry about being in constant control.* Too many deals die because one party (usually the seller) can't or won't give up control. The seller controls the company up until closing. The buyer controls it after closing. During the month before and the few months after closing, collaboration takes precedence.

A buy-sell deal is a short-term partnership, but it is a partnership nonetheless. That means most of this section is mental. If you approach it as a partnership versus a win-lose transaction, the chances of success escalate.

Players or Plays?
It's About the People

Players or play? Every professional sports team—be it baseball, basketball, football, soccer, or hockey—has the same plays. So the outcome is decided by how well the players execute those plays. Or how they adjust when the other team does something to stymie the original play.

Writers or stories? A great story carries itself. But what about the other 99.9% (of stories)? A good writer makes a story come alive, also known as non-fiction. A great writer creates her own story, aka fiction. Many of the stories we know, love, and repeat would be nothing without a storyteller, i.e., a person.

People or technology/strategy? These thoughts came to me after a visit to one of my banks' ATM machines. Every time I go to one of their machines, the first message tells me they are "checking my preferences." Then they ask if I want to use English or Spanish. You'd think that if they really were checking my preferences they'd know I want to use English.

When I get cash, the screen shows two places to the right of the decimal. Yet the machine doesn't give out coins, or even $1, $5, or $10 bills. So why have those places to the right of the decimal (other banks don't)?

Because, as with the first two examples, it's the people. Someone writing code didn't take off the decimal places or actually have the system remember my preferences.

Strategies are a lot easier to formulate than execute. As with sports, there are very few, if any, new strategies. They do change over time as technology—not just "high tech"—changes, but it takes the right people to implement the strategy

When it comes time to buy or sell a business, pay attention to the people around you, as they are the key to the company, its future success, and the deal. Both sides need to pay attention to the people, specifically:

- *Employees.* In a perfect world, the employees would be one big happy family, striving for the common good, always doing what needs to be done. But it's not a perfect world, and this is the reason why every business publication is filled with articles on management styles, motivation, leadership, etc. Besides employees, the other important people are:

- *Customers.* Everybody's (buyers, appraisers, banks) first question is, "What's the customer concentration?" Just as important—maybe even more important—is: How loyal are the customers? What other options do they have? What prices are the top customers paying? How fast do top customers pay. A loyal customer who pays a fair price, pays on time, and has limited options can outweigh many concentration concerns. Of course, if they are loyal because of price and have other options, it exaggerates the concentration issue.

- *Vendors.* A banker friend told me her bank almost didn't make a loan to a company because that company had a serious vendor concentration issue. The bank did due diligence on the vendor. If the vendor ran into problems, their loan would have problems. This means, have a variety of vendors and options.

- *Competitors.* Know the competitive landscape. Some industries are ruthless, others friendly. I've had bankers tell me they like having other bankers in networking groups so they know who to trust when they can't help someone. I've had clients refer business back and forth with companies whose services overlap a little. I just met an owner wanting to sell who was referred by a friendly competitor whose Venn diagram overlapped about 25% with my client.

The old maxim "putting people first" couldn't be more applicable to buying or selling a business. After all, you need to know who's minding the store and who's bringing in the bread.

Chapter 32

Pride in Ownership/Your Biz

I've noticed that owners of what I call micro-businesses, sales of $250,000 to $500,000 and even up to $1 million, often take more pride in what they've built than owners whose companies have broken through and are doing $5 million, $10 million, $20 million, or more.

Talk to owners of a micro-business, and you will hear immense satisfaction in their voices about what they've done. They tell stories about how they help their customers and about the jobs they've created, which allow their employees to support their families.

I'm not saying owners of larger-sized small businesses aren't proud. As I see regularly, when it comes time to sell, owners of larger firms are just as attached to their "baby" as owners of micro-businesses. I just don't see them as demonstrative about what they've done. They talk more about process, products or marketing than the intangibles.

I'm not sure why, and I don't know if there needs to be a reason. At all levels, founders and owners (and CEOs) should be proud of what they've accomplished. We know there are enough people not in business who don't understand what it takes to build a company. (Many of these people work in government.)

Part of this may be because these micro-business owners are not really businesspeople. They have a skill they turned into a business. Maybe they saw the niche, maybe they didn't like working for someone else, or perhaps they wanted to be in control, for better or for worse. Buyers like this, because buyers usually have skills in business processes, management and leadership. They want to grow something, and they see the opportunity to turn a good business into a great business.

What does this mean to business buyers and sellers? To buyers, it means you have to show respect for what the seller has done. Their business is a reflection of themselves. An easy trap to fall into when looking at a business is to find all of the things "wrong" with it. But every business has issues, aka blemishes, from the largest companies like Apple, Boeing, car manufacturers and others to small mom-and-pop enterprises.

Profits show the business has overcome their blemishes. They've found a way to make money in spite of not being perfect. As emphasized in other places in this book, a big part of how they do this is the people. Many employees of small businesses could make more money at a larger firm. But they don't want to be treated as a number. They want to be treated as a person, they want flexibility, and they want to see their direct contribution.

Sellers, keep in mind the following statement from a business buyer to a seller, when the seller didn't want the buyer to meet the company's key people before closing: "You may think I'm buying your company, but I'm really buying your people."

You've created jobs, provided benefits, been there during their tough times, and created advancement opportunities. Let the buyer know how good your people are. Encourage your employees to take pride in the business, come up with ideas, and stimulate growth.

As a seller, you expect the buyer to have the same passion for "your" business as you do. As a buyer, when you have that passion (and see where you can add value), you've found your match.

Chapter 33

Park your Ego at the Door!

By Robert L. Hild, CEO, ACT Capital Advisors, LLC

Yeah, I get it—it's your baby. You birthed it. You managed it through the terrible twos. You nurtured it through childhood. You hung on for dear life during adolescence. And now it's time to marry her off to someone you hardly know.

You deserve to be proud of the company you created. You put in all the hard work and sleepless nights to get her ready for this big day. You took the risks when no one else would. You know the company inside and out. There is nothing you cannot do, and probably no one who can do it better than you.

But you know that your baby isn't perfect. She has her flaws, some of your own making. However, it is hard to hear that from a near-stranger, and you'll be dammed if you're going to sit back while someone criticizes her or your parenting style. It's hard not to be a mama bear.

Negotiating the sale of your company is contentious by nature. Both parties are attempting to negotiate in their best interests. For you, as the seller, it can become personal. It is hard to hear about your baby's flaws, even if you are aware of them.

It is important to understand the nature of the game you are playing and your role in it. You and your M&A advisor are working to maximize value. To do so requires showing your company in the best light. The buyer's role is to pay as little as possible. To better understand the risks and costs associated with the weakness, the buyer will drill down into them and factor them into the purchase price. This is no different than selling your home and the buyer finds deferred maintenance that needs to be fixed. In most cases you reduce the purchase price and let the buyer deal with the repairs.

Businesses are no different. Business-buying can also be less about value, and in this case more about attempting to acquaint oneself with what one is purchasing, where the opportunities for growth are, and what areas of the company need shoring up. During the business-buying process it's easy for the seller to take offense at the buyer's intentional or unintentional comments, but that is not conducive to completing a transaction.

I've seen many good deals get derailed because of something the buyer said about the company that offended the owner. And trust me, it will happen. I have found that the following helps clients through the process:

1. *Stay focused on the objective.* This is about selling your company at the highest and best value, which will provide you the financial freedom to pursue the things that matter most to you.

2. *Keep it in context.* This is a contentious process, each side attempting to achieve opposing objectives. If the tables were reversed, you would be asking the same questions.

If you can understand in advance that this is naturally a contentious process and you can successfully set aside your ego, you are more likely to complete the transaction and move on to the next chapter in your life.

Robert Hild
ACT Capital Advisors
RHild@actcapitaladvisors.com

Chapter 34

When Buying a Franchise Warrants Consideration by an Entrepreneur

By Curt M. Maier, MBA, CMAI, CFB, Vice President of Business Development, International Business Associates

A SuperBroker is a professional intermediary with the ability to facilitate deals involving established businesses and sell new franchise business opportunities. As a SuperBroker holding licenses to sell both existing businesses and prospective franchises, I first present businesses in my inventory to buyers, and if a match cannot be located I enable an entrepreneur to move forward with a franchise purchase from a vetted list. Here are four conditions under which a franchise warrants consideration:

1. **Location.** One significant advantage of starting a business or buying a franchise is location selection. Motivations for placing a business in a specific area can range from identifying a community need to wanting to be close to home.

2. **Industry.** An entrepreneur's success depends largely on experience, knowledge, and ability. The resume of a potential entrepreneur will have a lifetime of accumulated experience. It makes sense to use this experience as an entrepreneur. Finding a business to purchase in the right location that uses this experience can be problematic. One solution is to buy a franchise in an appropriate industry. Quality franchises exist in almost every industry.

3. **Opportunity.** Successful entrepreneurship requires identifying an opportunity and executing a business plan to acquire market share and generate a return on investment. Franchises offer an opportunity to bring a new product

or service into a community employing a proven business model. Franchises also provide entrepreneurs with the advantages of their research and development without having to burden the costs associated with the process. Many wonderful ideas are never brought to market or able to be executed profitably. In addition, significant financial rewards are often received by the first company to introduce a product or service to a group of customers.

4. **Support.** The transition from corporate or military employee to entrepreneur can be daunting. Whether you're working for a company or serving in the military, there is always someone with more experience available to ask questions and assist on a project beyond your skill set. There are also people available with diverse knowledge and experience who are responsible for elements of business operations outside of your area of focus. A franchisor offers a similar infrastructure of support to franchisees. A franchisor trains each franchisee on how to effectively operate the business model and has support individuals in place to help with business issues such as facility leasing, tenant improvement buildouts, equipment purchasing and leasing, website design, advertising, etc. This support system can make the difference between success and failure for a first-time entrepreneur.

The rewards of entrepreneurship are significant for a person willing to take the risk who has the ability to execute successfully. Acquiring a mature, profitable business is regarded as the lowest-risk entry point into entrepreneurship. However, if a business in the right industry and location cannot be acquired, the next best option for a motivated individual is to buy a franchise.

Curt M. Maier
IBA
(425) 505-3649
curt@ibainc.com

Sell the Right Business

We're on track to closing, only to find out we're on the wrong track. After the usual disruptions of illness, food poisoning, and the seller falling off a ladder, things came to a halt when it was discovered that the PSA was for the wrong company.

You're probably thinking something like, "How the heck can *that* happen?" Well it has to do with Canadian tax law, and there's no real correlation to U.S. tax law, so, as you probably live or work in the U.S., just enjoy the story and pay attention to the related points.

Canada had, at least at the time of the deal, a one-time capital-gains exemption for selling the stock of a privately held business. So it behooves the seller to take advantage of this. It also behooves the buyer to do so, because if the seller keeps more of the price, more price flexibility results.

With only the lease to be finalized, someone discovered that the contract was for selling the operating entity, not the parent (holding) company. Bye-bye, tax exemption.

To make this even more humorous, the original draft of the agreement had it correct, but the seller's mergers-and-acquisitions attorney changed it. Oops! And I'm guessing a lot of donated time to make the correction.

This story, while entertaining, brings up an important point. There's a reason for all of the minutiae involved in a buy-sell deal: something done years ago can come back to haunt you. Something you thought was handled properly wasn't. The 1% of shares given to an employee or family member has to be accounted for.

The last point above is critical if the buyer is using an SBA-guaranteed loan to finance the acquisition. The buyer must purchase 100% of the company, and sellers can't work for the company for more than one year, at least in writing. This means the majority owner must buy any employee-owned shares before the deal closes.

One thing that often creeps into to the works is an old loan or lease that has been paid off for years and the bank or equipment dealer "forgot" to remove the lien. Don't worry about the State or the IRS. They blatantly make it known when they even think they are owed money.

A few years ago, a deal died over an IRS lien. The seller wouldn't take responsibility for it, wouldn't put money in escrow for it. Since tax issues transcend a sale, stock or asset structure, no way was the buyer going to do the deal.

Loose ends can delay or even kill the deal. This is also why there are lien checks and checks with the State to make the sure the company is registered correctly, the company owns the name, the seller legally owns the business, etc.

The last thing a buyer wants is to find out post-sale that she doesn't have the legal rights she thought she had. And getting tangled in a messy web post-sale is the last thing the seller wants. Neither side wants the associated legal bills. The costs to do it correctly upfront are far less than the costs of fixing it later.

My advice is to sell (and buy) the right company, do it the right way, and handle all the minutiae.

Chapter 36

Searching is an Ongoing Game

I like to say that searching for a business or a buyer of your business is a contact sport. The more contacts you make, the better the odds of finding a good match.

There are only three ways to search, whether it's to buy or sell a business, to find a job, or to find customers. You can:

1. Go to the public market—advertising sites, intermediaries, etc.

2. Network, network, and network even more.

3. Be proactive—pick up the phone.

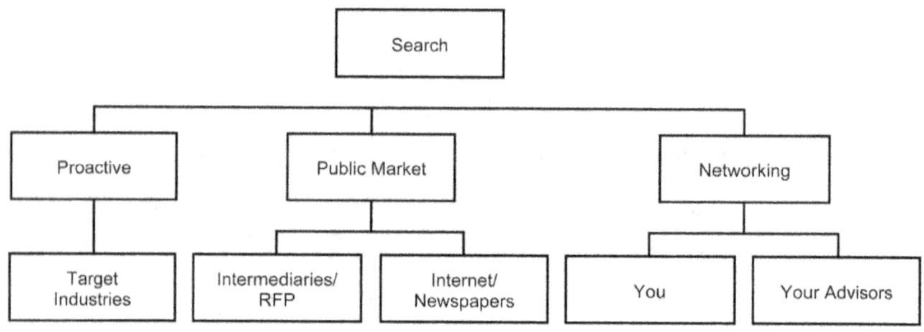

The above is for any type of search– buyer, seller, finding customers, or finding a job– and it's pretty obvious (at least to me). Where it falls apart is the execution, so let's look at where and why it falls apart.

On the buyer side, my best client was one who did all of the above with maximum effort and had a deal five months after we started. (I tell buyers to allow at least nine to twelve months.) I couldn't go to an event and not see this client. He followed up regularly with every intermediary, and was aggressive on the proactive side.

This is the opposite of most buyers, who seem to wait for the phone to ring. They're not out in the community. They expect the intermediaries to call them, and they micromanage any outreach to companies. (Remember, 50-80% of small-to-mid-sized businesses are never advertised for sale.) Buyers need to be aggressive, because most deals are in an industry the buyer never thought of before seeing the business they end up buying.

With sellers, it's inaction, due to one important word: confidentiality—or should I say the fear of a confidentiality breach (see the chapter on this topic). They've heard horror stories from friends whose employees, customers, or competitors found out they were for sale. So, they sit and wait, sometimes until it's too late.

Doing all the right things is a start, but you must also do them the right *way*. Here are some tips:

Be consistent and constant. This means having a plan and always executing it.

Know what you're going to communicate. Be open, honest, friendly, and cheerful.

When you find a good match, do all you can to move it along.

One of my favorite stories is: I was having coffee with a buyer and a seller. They wanted to do a deal but kept stumbling. I said to the buyer, "Good businesses are hard to find, so when you find a good one that fits your skills, and you like the owner, get the deal done." I told the seller, "It's tough to find a qualified buyer with money, and whom you like. When you find one, get the deal done." They got the message, got over the hump, and closed in six weeks.

You may have to kiss a lot of frogs to get the prince—i.e., see a lot of buyers or businesses before making a decision—but it's worth it when you find the right one.

Chapter 37

Buyers: Don't Be Too Fussy

Most business buyers are too fussy. I remind all buyers that there are no perfect businesses or deals, so be alert for anything that looks good.

No small business saves the world or changes western civilization. But these businesses do create jobs, wealth, and a lifestyle for both the employees and the owner. Keeping that in mind, buyers need to answer the following three questions:

- Can you see yourself going in there every day?

- Can you add value?

- Is it a viable business model, i.e. it has a future, that doesn't violate your values?

The rest is analysis, due diligence, negotiation, etc. And, on the flipside to the seller underestimating the complexity of the process, the buyer must realize that it's OK to ask another question, because the buyer needs to get over that impulse to snub an imperfect opportunity by making a hasty decision. As I wrote in the preface to *Buying A Business That Makes You Rich*, and have reiterated throughout this book, buyers will make a leap of faith, and it needs to be off a chair, not the roof.

But how do you know if a business is for you? Let's start with three considerations:

1. *Start at the 30,000-foot level instead of getting caught in the weeds.* Do you like the business, the industry, the owner's role, etc.?

2. *What do you want to do on a daily, weekly and monthly basis?* My friend Keith likes to make things. His company makes products for the outdoor enthusiast, and I'll bet he would be just as happy making indoor products; he likes the manufacturing and distribution process. Other buyers/owners like the team building aspect or the customer contact. Know what you want to do to add value.

3. *To buy and own a business, you must have the skills to manage people, processes, money, and enthusiasm.* Where are you on a 1-10 scale on each of these? This will influence your decision.

Use the following chart to guide your decision as to why you want to buy a business and what you want to do.

	1-10 scale	Rank
Be the boss		
Benefit personally from my intelligent and hard work		
Control		
Creativity		
Decision-maker		
Equity or net worth		
Flexibility		
Income potential		
Independence		
FUN		

There is no right or wrong, although, in my opinion, if money is the main reason for wanting to own a business, you will not enjoy it as much as if independence, fun and putting your own twist on things (being creative) are your top reasons. (Not that money isn't important, of course.)

The bottom line is, don't get into the weeds on what the business makes, sells or services. People with micro-retail businesses get into them because of the product. Do what you'll enjoy.

Catastrophe to Owner, Not Business

Business owners/sellers, this is what buyers are looking for: Owners hit by catastrophic events that happened to them personally, not to their businesses.

This creates urgency, and since statistics have shown that only about 10% of small- and mid-sized businesses are prepared for a sale, the chances are that the catastrophe will hurt (the selling price). The usual suspects are start with the three Ds—divorce, death, and disability. I've seen divorces force a sale (and actually worked on one). I've seen estates sell the business, and owners whose health was so bad they had to sell. Let's expand upon what happens when the owner dies.

Case 1: Owner dies, son moves up from shop foreman to president, business suffers, and about a year and a half later the company isn't worth buying for more than the liquidation value of the assets. No plan, no management team, and they should have sold immediately.

Case 2: Owner has long illness, dies, husband who's retired keeps it going and gets some nice distributions—and actually says, "I sign all the checks so the employees think I'm paying attention to the business." But with no adult supervision, there's no emphasis on growth. Pretty soon the inattention takes its toll, and the business sells for very little money down plus an earnout. And then there's divorce:

Case 3: Couple is getting divorced and the spouse wants cash not a share of the business. This happened as the business was experiencing a down part of the business cycle. It sold for one-third of what had been offered a few years prior, during an up part of the cycle.

Realistically, the three Ds don't happen that often. What happens is usually one of the following seven reasons, in order based on my experience. Understand that there's very little difference in preparation for the three Ds or the following reasons for selling—meaning almost no preparation—in most cases.

Burnout. Management and executive-level people are reported to change jobs every 3-7 years. Business owners are a little better. It takes them 15-20 years (or more) to burn out and need a change. Then there are the owners who started working at Dad's company when they were 13, and by the time they're 55 they can't stand it anymore. A friend sold his third-generation company and said he was so glad to not have to worry about all the little things anymore after 40 years of it.

Retirement. If the owner is in his or her 80s, there's a very good chance they'll die at their desk. They have no life outside of business. Most sell to retire between 60 and early 70s. Owners, pick the exit date and plan for it. If you stay longer, great—the business is still ready.

Health. It could be the owner's health or the spouse's. It could be serious, or simply a warning shot (to slow down). Buyers, you may not find out about this until due diligence. The seller won't want to appear to be overly motivated. On one deal, the spouse had a medical episode during diligence, and then we found out the owner also had some health issues.

Life. To paraphrase the old bumper sticker, "Life Happens." All the more reason for owners to prepare the business for sale, because "life happens" means a surprise could pop up at any time.

Business outgrows owner. As in, "I got into this to design widgets, and now I manage a few dozen people, and I don't like managing people." A darn good reason to sell.

Dispute. When partners fight, stay clear. One owner said the business was worth $X million. I asked if he would buy out his partner for half X. He said, "No, I'll pay him one-quarter X." It was best to just sell the whole thing.

Entrepreneurism. Related to burnout, the owner has an idea for a new business and can't do both. He or she is (obviously) more motivated to play with the new one, so it's bye-bye existing one. (See 'Burnout,' above.)

Chapter 39

Show Growth and Prove It

Here are three examples that show how growth takes effort:

1. I recently conducted a valuation for a small company doing under $1 million in sales. We also had a client doing $10 million in sales that had the same issue as the small firm; their facilities were both at capacity. Their options included adding a second shift and getting more space. But you don't just add a shift. It takes management, admin support, and, depending on the level of business access to parts, tools or similar, it's not simple. Getting more space means a medium to long-term commitment on a lease, plus hiring more people. You should have potential business in the queue, or it could get expensive. A buyer got a fantastic deal after an owner expanded into a new market (with the costs of space and people), struggled, and was forced to sell by the State Department of Revenue.

2. Years ago I helped a company that was unsalable. It was a nice business model, but the owner had an outside interest, which was horse-training. When business was good, he spent more time with the horses. When business declined, he would focus on the business. This up-and-down cycle went on for years, resulting in an underwater balance sheet, because the ups didn't cover the downs and the resultant debt kept growing. We put in a marketing and sales plan, monitored weekly activity, and, after six months, sales exceeded budget by 33%. Six months later, a strategic buyer

made an offer, and the owner turned it down, because business was now fun. Five years later, the same buyer came back with a much larger offer, which was accepted.

3. Six months after acquiring a business, a buyer shared that sales were up, his salesperson was great, and, "It's amazing what happens when you actually pick up the phone and call your customers." Coasting businesses take orders; growth-oriented businesses take action. This buyer would have paid more for the business had the seller called the customers.

The important takeaways from the second story include:

- Have a plan.

- Monitor it.

- The marketing and sales departments have to work together.

- It takes work.

- Oh, and it pays off, as in the third story.

Just as important is to document all of your business activities and know why certain ones didn't work. If for no other reason, it keeps new employees from wanting to reinvent things.

Marketing and sales are the obvious ways to grow and must be done constantly. What else?

- **New product lines.** A buyer with industry experience started making calls to suppliers during due diligence. He lined up new product lines to expand the service offerings in the first month of his business ownership.

- **Outside reps.** If it works for your business, you can grow on a pure commission basis.

- **Do great work.** Not just good work—*great* work. Your customers will tell others.

- **Buy another company.** The last chapter in this book, a section from my book *Company Growth By Acquisition Makes Dollars & Sense*, covers 19 reasons to consider growth by acquisition. Give serious thought to this strategy, especially when other businesses are struggling. I'm writing and publishing this book during the COVID-19 crisis, which has hurt a lot of businesses. So growth by acquisition may be a company's best option, especially when an individual buyer won't want to buy it (little to no profits), and perhaps there's even a job for the seller.

To reiterate the chapter title: When you can show growth, prove it, and share how it was achieved. Then you're in a stronger selling position and more attractive to buyers.

Overleverage Will Kill You

A *Wall Street Journal* article discussed the Japanese company Suntory and its 2014 acquisition of Jim Beam. One of the most interesting comments was:

To help pay back debt amassed in the deal—one of the biggest-ever overseas transactions by a Japanese company—Suntory is trying to double global spirits sales by 2020. Hitting that goal won't be easy. Suntory will have to outpace industrywide growth in its two biggest markets, the U.S. and Japan, and expand into new markets.

Wow! The acquirer wants to or has to double sales in five years in a competitive market and exceed industry trends (a trend where whiskey was on the upswing, and which could change at any time) to cover their debt. My first three thoughts are:

- They paid too much.

- They leveraged the deal too highly.

- Where was the common sense?

Let's step back from the large corporate acquisitions and concentrate on the traps that buyers (and sellers) face in the small-to-mid-size buy-sell market.

It's awfully easy for buyers to pay way too much when there's a (perceived) shortage of companies for sale, easy money, and parties who think only about the dollars today. The bottom line is, if like Suntory, you have to significantly grow the company to cover your debt. Well, you paid too much.

So who lends on deals like this? Nobody in *my* market! Banks have ratios, guidelines, and regulators. This means it's non-bank money, and I'm sure the interest rates are a lot higher. Is the risk worth it? We'll find out, won't we? I saw how Al's Soups (the store made famous by *Seinfeld's* "Soup Nazi" episode) needed more capital because they didn't have enough cash. Sears was and is constantly running out of cash as their turnaround is failing. It doesn't always work out, per the young analyst's spreadsheet.

The above two paragraphs make my point about, "Where was the common sense?" It's easy to say greed overcame common sense, but these are not stupid people making these deals. So maybe it's ego, career advancement (nobody ever thinks their deal will fail and their career will be doomed), or overconfidence in the desire to impress shareholders.

The above is just financial. As *The Wall Street Journal* points out:

At the same time, another challenge looms: meshing two vastly different corporate cultures inside its new global liquor subsidiary.

Time for another "Wow!" In my small business deals the change in culture is usually the employees saying the buyer is a "breath of fresh air." They welcome the opportunity to be listened to, be creative, and see career advancement.

If the deal seems too good to be true, it probably is. Having to double sales in five years to cover debt payments means it's pretty risky. Of course, in the above case, it's not the decision-makers personal money, as it is in the small business world, and it's not the seller getting caught in the mess, or getting the company back, if she agrees to an overleveraged deal.

Chapter 41

Lease Issues

Let's start with a basic fact: It's rare for a bank to give a business buyer a loan for a term longer than the term of the lease, including options. It might happen for an office-based business, but it won't happen for retail, manufacturing, distribution, or even service (if they stock inventory, have a lot of vehicles, etc.). A smart buyer will realize that, if a bank won't do the deal without a good lease, why should the buyer? Who wants to be forced to move in the middle of making acquisition payments?

So, what's worse?

- A landlord happy with a month-to-month arrangement.

- A landlord seeking to take advantage of the buyer.

- The property scheduled to be redeveloped for a more profitable use.

- The offer of a "short" lease to see how the buyer works out.

Actually, it's all of the above. Don't discount the lease and its effect on closing the deal. An eight-figure deal was delayed (and we know what can happen the longer things go) because the seller didn't want to approach the landlord of 20+ years. Of course, the landlord was fine with a new long-term lease.

Or the seller who put her head in the sand over an upcoming move (for redevelopment of the property) and said, "It will be the buyer's issue." No, it's *your* issue. What made this more interesting was that the estimated cost of the move was at least one year's profit (into seven figures plus the cost of employee attrition).

What are the things to watch out for?

- *Timing is everything.* A deal contains a lot of moving parts, which often leads to contingencies. The buyer doesn't want to be committed to the lease until the deal closes but the deal can't close until she has a lease.

- *A boilerplate lease taken from the Internet or a textbook.* They tend to cause more problems and higher legal bills than they think they're solving by being simple, generic, and untailored to the uniqueness of the situation.

- *An onerous lease.* This is one no sane tenant would sign.

- An example: The business seller constructed a building, after a few years sold it to an investor, signed a ridiculous lease holding him responsible for everything (foundation, walls, etc.), and did so because he built and knew the building. Fast-forward 10-15 years, and he's selling the business. The landlord wants the same lease, the buyer and his attorney say, "No way," and the seller has to move the business to facilitate the sale.

A real estate professional can give you more details and more traps to avoid. In some situations the buyer may be able to have the lease assigned to him by the landlord. This may be the best alternative, if it meets bank criteria.

Your facilities are a big part of a company's growth potential. If you are bursting at the seams, what are the buyer's options? If you have 20,000 square feet and need 10,000 more, what does that mean to a buyer who also has to make acquisition debt payments? Can you add a second shift? Does a remote location make sense? What about zoning limitations? All of these will be of concern to a buyer, so have a handle on them.

A landlord's willingness to assign the lease or give a buyer a new one at a fair rate is also important. The supply and demand for the type of space your company needs is one of the biggest factors in all of this. If supply is tight, a landlord can play tough. If supply greatly exceeds demand, the landlord will do everything possible to keep the business as a tenant.

Chapter 42

Commercial Lease Considerations for Both Parties to a Business Transaction

**By Dean Altaras, CCIM, and Billy Poll, CCIM,
Partners, NAI-Puget Sound Properties**

In the sale or transfer of a business, an assignment of its current lease is one of the transaction's key components. If a new lease cannot be negotiated directly with the landlord, the assignment will act to transfer the leasehold interest and obligations from one tenant (here, the business seller) to another (the business buyer).

Managing the lease assignment must begin early in the sale process. Principal tenets for consideration by both parties are:

ASSIGNOR—THE ORIGINAL TENANT (SELLER OF BUSINESS)

- Determine how the lease rent obligation impacts the value of the business, as this is a fixed expense that cannot be modified.

- Make sure adequate time remains on the lease term, as a minimal term could adversely affect the value of your business. A significant part of what you are selling is a leasehold interest in a physical location.

- Be certain that the current lease can indeed be assigned, and confirm the timelines and processing costs associated with obtaining the landlord's approval.

- Contact the landlord immediately to communicate your intentions around selling your business and assigning your lease to avoid delays when seeking the landlord's approval.

- Remember that, from the landlord's perspective, an assignment is often viewed as a lateral move and a nuisance, whereby the landlord continues to collect the same rent, but possibly from an unproven tenant.

- Confirm that any options to extend the lease are transferable to the buyer of the business.

- Understand any ongoing lease liability you may have after the assignment and sale are closed.

- If this option is available, encourage a new lease directly between the landlord and the buyer of the business, thus removing yourself from any ongoing liability under the current lease.

ASSIGNEE—THE NEW TENANT (BUYER OF BUSINESS)

- Obtain a copy of the lease agreement as soon as possible, and confirm that the lease can be assigned or transferred.

- Confirm that any options and/or rights of first refusal to extend the lease or purchase the property are assignable.

- Understand any lease conditions that may require additional financial commitments, such as personal guaranties and lease deposits.

- Make sure that adequate time remains on the lease, to ensure the ongoing viability of the purchased business.

- Ensure that the lease is assignable to a third party, in the event that the business is sold again, and request that the landlord's consent will be granted in a short period of time and shall not be unreasonably withheld or delayed.

- Request, and possibly require, an option to extend the lease, preferably with a pre-negotiated rent structure for the purposes of cash flow planning and, if not, fair market rent with an arbitration clause.

- If appropriate and available, request an option to purchase or a right of first refusal to purchase the property.

Dean Altaras CCIM, Partner & Billy Poll, CCIM, Partner
NAI-Puget Sound Properties
daltaras@nai-psp.com   425-586-5613
bpoll@nai-psp.com   425-586-5604

Chapter 43

Value is in the Eye of the Beholder; Show it to them

It's rare to see a write-up (memorandum, prospectus, etc.) of a business that isn't filled with fluff and hyperbole about the business, how great everything is, how much greater it will be with a new owner, etc., etc. While private equity firms have a love affair with "the book," as they call it, other buyers often dismiss it as mostly marketing.

On the flipside, individual buyers (executives) tend to strut around with a resume filled with business-school lingo most sellers don't understand. Sellers don't care about that stuff. They want to know if the buyer can make the payments, take care of the employees, and maintain the legacy.

Here are some tips, for both buyers and sellers:

- *Present yourself well, and talk sense.* In your first meeting buyers shouldn't claim to know how you would grow the business. Nor should sellers talk about how much potential the business has if they haven't been exploiting said potential.

- *Tell stories.* Sellers, give examples of how you came through for a customer in a crisis situation or how your team blew it and ultimately recovered. This is what buyers want to hear. Tell and show the marketing strategies you used and what they did for your business. It's powerful to say things like, "Three years ago we put in a new sales plan, started using a CRM, monitored our salespeople's activity, and since then we've grown 12% annually, versus 3% prior to this."

- *Give specific examples.* A buyer needs to tell, in detail, how she revamped the purchasing department, streamlined ordering, tied purchasing to estimating, and reduced material costs by 14% over two years. Saying you can do something is one thing; giving concrete examples is another.

- *Don't be afraid to boast, but be able to back it up.* Especially in these days of social media and the Internet, just about everything is verifiable ("trust, but verify" comes to mind). One of my favorite examples is a client for whom we determined the root cause of the situation: an offering price lower than what the owner wanted led to inconsistent revenues. After working on it for a year, we were able to tell buyers:

  We determined a need to stabilize and grow revenues. The first step was to create a marketing outreach plan to past, current and potential customers. We then executed the marketing with follow-up sales efforts starting a week later. It was essential for us to track every piece of mail, email, and phone call. After three months, we had enough information to know what worked best. After six months, sales were 150% of projections, and this growth continued for the next six months. The 12-month time period had record sales and profits, and this continued for at least three more years.

- Ask good questions, you'll be respected for it.

I could easily give you more stories for both buyers and sellers, but I think you get the point. Give examples, tell stories, don't be bashful—and of course, tell the truth.

Chapter 44

The Magic Question

Simplicity is often the best course of action. In fact, Ockham's Razor, attributed to English philosopher and theologian William of Ockham in the 14th century, states that one should solve problems by choosing the solution that makes the fewest assumptions.

In the case of buying and selling a business, there has to be a match between the skills and interests of the buyer and the seller. And it goes a lot deeper.

The following simple little question to the seller uncovers at least five issues or opportunities: "What does the seller do on a daily, weekly and monthly basis?" Let's examine this.

Skills match. This question lets the buyer know if there's a match between the duties she wants to perform and what the seller does—or should I say, what the seller *needs* to do. An overly analytical, introverted person may love the business model, but if the owner is a key component of the sales team and process, it's probably not a good fit. Correspondingly, the outgoing "I want to be in front of customers" buyer isn't a good fit for a business requiring attention to detail on bids, contracts, job prototypes, etc.

Dependency. In my talks I say to audiences, "You have a dependency on the owner if you can fill in the blank with statements like, 'If the owner is the only one who can _________________:

- Program the machine;

- Make the big sales;

- Approve all bids'."

Most people think of dependencies in terms of customer concentration, but in small businesses it's what the owner does or doesn't do that often makes a difference. Buyers want owners who can take off for three weeks and return to a company in as good of or better shape as when they left.

'In' versus 'on.' The buyer wants an owner who works "on" the business versus "in" the business. Working *on* the business means strategy, growth, vision, etc. Working *in* the business means being on the shop floor, making sales calls, doing bids, etc. While on the surface it may look like opportunity if the buyer can add strategy and vision, in the short-term it means hiring someone to do the day-to-day tasks that are eating up the seller's day. It's the difference between having a job as company president and having a job as an employee.

Lifestyle business. My favorite story concerns the owner (seller) who told the buyer how he and his sales team worked just hard enough to make the income they wanted and didn't work anymore. He lost a great buyer who figured that changing the culture of laziness to one of growth would alienate the employees, and he would lose them. This was a lifestyle business—and there are a lot of them.

No number two. Just like on Star Trek Next Generation, you have to have a good number two (employee). Actually, when we say, "No number two person is a red flag," what we're really saying is, there's no management team. It ties into the above reasons, because it means the owner is integral to the day-to-day operations and works in the business, and this is probably not what the buyer wants in a business.

That simple little question, "What does the seller do on a daily, weekly and monthly basis?", opens up a plethora of information.

Chapter 45

The Alphabet Soup of Earnings Terminology

Profit, EBITDA, SDE, recast income, free cash flow, and other terms bounce around the buy-sell industry like a racquetball in a fast-paced game. What's worse is that these terms are often defined differently. Let's take a look at them, what they really mean, and how to apply them. Because, no matter what, no matter how a valuation methodology is applied, in a buy-sell deal it comes down to a return on investment (ROI), and using one term versus another can create drastically different results.

'**Profit.**' I like to say, if businesses operated to maximize income instead of paying less in taxes, we would get a truer picture of a company's income viability. Small-business reporting is not like public-company reporting, where the public company wants to show maximum income to encourage an increase in its stock price. Business owners strive to minimize taxes, so the profit figure on the income statement or the tax return is rarely valid.

'**Recast profit.**' Adjusting for non-business expenses or singular events gives a much better indication of a company's status. A singular event could be a once-in-20-years expense for a new HVAC system or a one-time, large order that won't occur again. It allows a buyer and a lender to know what the buyer's available cash will be. This often is a very valid figure.

'**EBITDA.**' The acronym stands for "earnings before interest, taxes, depreciation, and amortization." This is supposed to give an indication of true cash flow, because, in theory, depreciation and amortization are noncash expenses, and interest is included because a buyer may have different financing than the current owner. However, EBITDA doesn't make allowances for Section 179 and other accelerated depreciation deductions, anticipated capital expenditures, or the cost of working capital, which for many businesses is a critical and needed expense. As with adjusted profit, you must allow for a fair-market salary for the owner. EBITDA is a corporate term, and you don't see public companies adjust and add back management salaries to profits.

'Seller's discretionary earnings.' This is often EBITDA plus owner's salary. The theory is that all money to an owner is discretionary, and it's the owner's decision to take a salary, use the money to grow the business, or pay acquisition debt. Owner compensation is not—repeat, not—discretionary. I suspect it came about because brokers got sick of arguing about what the fair-market salary for a business's owner should be. In reality, for almost all owners and buyers, a salary to support their personal life is not discretionary. An appraiser (and banker) will always allow for a fair-market salary, because, if the owner decides to not be active, someone will get paid to do that job. In my opinion, the term 'seller's discretionary earnings' is usually inappropriate, and it loses all effectiveness once a business's adjusted profit plus salary reaches $500,000.

'Free cash flow.' In simple terms, take EBITDA (including the adjusted profit figure that allows for a fair-market owner salary) and deduct anticipated capital expenditures and operating interest (not acquisition interest). This is a figure I see sophisticated buyers zero in on, especially in these days of complicated and changing accelerated depreciation schedules. It also gives a seller credit for recent large capital expenditures that will reduce the buyer's need for upcoming capital expenditures.

The above is why when someone says, "I want 5X for my business" or "I'll pay 4X for that company." My first question is, "4X (or 5X) of what?" Define the terms clearly to avoid future confusion.

Chapter 46

Working Capital Adjuster

It's always a project to determine how much working capital stays in the business after closing. With micro businesses, there isn't any. But for small, mid-sized and middle-market deals, the buyer should get the needed amount of working capital to be operational on day one.

The typical transaction structure is what's called "cash free/debt free" with a working capital adjuster. What exactly does this mean? Here are the bullet points followed by some explanation.

1. "Cash free/debt free" means the seller keeps the cash and pays off all the debt.

2. Working capital is typically accounts receivable plus inventory less accounts payable and accrued liabilities. (The current portion of long-term debt is not included.) Work in process and expenses in excess of billings, if any, also has to be factored into the formula.

3. The working capital target is the average over the trailing 12 months.

4. The final calculation is done post-close, usually 30-90 days after.

Point 1 is pretty straightforward unless there are deposits for future work. This could be a manufacturer or contractor getting 50% down and the rest upon delivery, or a collision repair shop getting a partial check from the insurance company at the start of the repair. If properly accounted for, the cash is deposited and credited to a deferred revenue account. Upon sale, the buyer should get cash to cover these deposits.

Point 2 gets interesting (i.e., confusing), especially when there is work in process. Part of this is the deferred revenue mentioned above. Another part, and always a moving target, is when costs in excess of billings arise. In other words, the company orders materials, has people working on the project, and hasn't billed the customer yet. These costs should go into a current asset account (and not expensed until billed). But small-business accounting does not always handle it this way.

To determine the target working capital that will remain in the company, an average over the previous 12 months is calculated. If actual working capital at closing is higher, the seller receives the difference. If lower, the seller pays the difference to the buyer. The theory is, the 12-month average is what is needed to run the business.

However, we rarely, if ever, know the exact amount at closing. Invoices are going out and coming in, deposits are made, checks are written and deposited, etc., as they normally are. So, after the books are closed, the target is calculated, the actual is known, and a true-up is done, usually within 60 days of closing. At this time other expenses and revenues are adjusted: pro rata rent, utilities, job billings crossing over the close date, etc.

Besides giving the buyer what she needs to run the business from day one, this adjuster also protects both sides. The buyer doesn't have to fear the seller accelerating A/R collections or delaying paying A/P. The seller doesn't have to worry about giving up too much if sales prior to closing are extremely high.

Chapter 47

Quality of Earnings

The old saying, "There's nothing new under the sun," doesn't apply to terminology. In recent years—i.e., in the last 10 or so—the term "Quality of Earnings Report" (QofE) has come into vogue. It's very prevalent in middle-market deals and has crept down to the lower-middle market and even below, especially in an extraordinary circumstance, such as a question or disagreement over how usable and salable the inventory is.

To me, a QofE is simply a mini-audit, but it sounds a lot nicer than anything with the word 'audit' in it. In simple terms, an independent accountant determines if the reported earnings are accurate and sustainable. One definition I've seen is "…a detailed analysis of all the components of a company's revenue and expenses."

For example, if earnings over the last couple of years are elevated because of the gain on the sale of assets, it's considered low quality of earnings. This is also true if sales volume stayed the same but commodity prices temporarily lowered, thus increasing margins and profits. In the latter case, when commodity prices increase, margins will decrease. Or, if it's a permanent decline market, prices may go down.

On the other hand, growth due to a marketing campaign, the sales team generating new customers, more productivity, or higher customer retention due to better service are all defined as high quality of earnings. In other words, internal improvements are of higher quality.

All this said, I've been encouraging all of this for years, without the QofE name. I've seen buyers bring in their CPA for a few days and others who have done most of their accounting themselves. Some of the work is basic, i.e., checking random bank statements, credit card bills, supplier invoices, etc. Much of it is asking the same questions any good due diligence effort would ask, but done by an independent third party.

A part of this should also be industry and economic research. To me, it's hard to do a report like this if you don't get to know the industry, which all good buyers will do on their own, including interviewing the sellers. A good report will include the accountant talking with the business owner and management team to find out the little intricacies on how the business operates, because every good small- to lower-middle-market company has its own special sauce. This is similar to what CPAs do for reviewed financial statements.

I've also seen some stupid questions. One time the question was partially intended as negotiation for the buyer when one of the accountants asked (and this showed a lack of independence), "Will the buyer's lease have them paying only the base rent as per the lease and not the other expenses?" Answer: No, the buyer will have a triple-net lease just like the seller. Another example is one person focusing on the bottom 10% of the customer base and asking why sales to those customers fluctuated year-to-year. I'd be more concerned with the top 10-20-30% of customers.

Finally, one buyer worried about customer concentration, as every year there was one customer with about 20% of sales, but it was a different customer every year, and over five years nothing came close to customer concentration.

The bottom line is: Business owners (sellers), don't be surprised if this comes up. In fact, if you're at the lower-middle-market level, I recommend you have a QofE done as part of your exit planning.

Chapter 48

Valuation

There are statistically backed-up ranges of value based on the size of the business, and to some extent the industry. We'll cover small and medium-sized and middle-market businesses (including those in the lower middle market), but not micro businesses like delis and dry-cleaners.

A couple of years ago I did a project for an attorney involved in a fraud case. It wasn't directly about his case, but about valuation ranges by size of business. Using a database of SBA business acquisition loans, I realized that, no matter how I manipulated the input, the average multiple of earnings for companies larger than micro business size and under $1.5 million of earnings (after fair-market owner compensation) was about 4X with a coefficient of variation of a little over 25%. This means the range for these businesses is 3-5X earnings.

Why the range? What I wrote in my report to the attorney was:

Two businesses in the same industry with the same sales and profits may be valued differently if, for example, one of them has:

- 80% of their sales to three customers and the other 80% of sales to 100 customers. Customer concentration is a huge risk and should scare every buyer, unless it's an add-on acquisition and is immediately reduced.

- So high a dependency on the owner that he can't take a vacation while the other has a solid management team.

- Been growing at 10-15% per year for five years, and the other has declining sales.

- No tangible assets to speak of, and the other is asset-heavy.

I also received information on middle-market deals from John O'Dore (see his essay in Chapter 21), and I wrote in my report, "Middle-market businesses that usually have profits over $1.5 million, and definitely over $2 million, typically sell for 5-10 times profit, depending on the size, industry, the above factors, etc. An even narrower range has companies with a value of under $100 million selling in the 6-8X range."

So, while there are exceptions, it's rare if a small and medium-sized business (SMB), one in the heart of the SBA loan scope, will sell for outside the 3-5X range. This means a rate of return on investment of 20-33%—a lot more than the long-term returns of the stock market, most real estate, etc., and it's lower because of the risk. Talking to one owner who thought the range mentioned here was too low, I simply asked him what would happen if one of his machines was down for a month. The answer was, "Big problems getting product to customers." I then asked him what would happen if a machine went down at his previous employer's ($500 million) company. He grudgingly said, "Not much." He got the point.

The ranges are valid, and it's all the other factors that determine where in the range the value lies. It comes down to the famous non-financial factors such as:

- Is there customer concentration or diversity?

- Are there indispensable employees (see Chapter 44, The Magic Question)?

- Is there adequate supplier diversity (no one key supplier)?

- What are the industry's competitive factors?

Conclusion: Valuation is an art as well as a science, and much of the art is knowing the market versus just using methodologies. Don't fall for any lines about how "special" or "un-special" the business is.

Chapter 49

Myths of Valuation

Whether you're a buyer or a seller, there are some fundamental "rules" and ever-present myths of valuation. Here are my top ones, and be aware that most, but not all, are present because they're used to increase the price of the business.

- *Owner compensation is the same as profit.* No matter what you see online, a broker tells you, owner comp is not discretionary, it's for the job of running the company. Business appraisers and bankers will put in a fair market salary for the job of CEO. Your mortgage payment isn't discretionary, is it?

- *Pay me for the cash I don't pay taxes on.* If someone has skimmed cash, i.e. cheated the IRS, they've already been paid for it. And, as my friend Ted Leverette (see his essay in chapter 51) told me, "What's worse, the owner who says he skims cash or the one who says he skims but really doesn't?" And it's not just restaurants and stores. A machine shop owner told me he sold his titanium scrap personally to the tune of six figures a year.

- *My $5 or $10 or $25 million business will sell for the same multiple as the $400 million-dollar business that recently sold.* As in a previous chapter, no, it won't because the $400 million-dollar company has more customers, management depth, backup equipment, etc.

- *The financial statements are all that matter.* As also aforementioned in this book, the non-financial factors are just as if not more important than the numbers. The numbers are history.

The customers, employees, management depth, suppliers, the competition, etc. tell you where the business is going, i.e. will the profits continue, grow, or decline.

- *I'll pay for the value of the assets, not blue sky.* It's a naïve buyer who thinks they'll get the business for book value. Buyers and banks should want a lot of goodwill because that means the value is based on the profits not the collateral. Blue sky means overpaying.

- *Pay me for the potential.* Buyers pay based on what the business has done. They buy it because they believe they can grow it (potential) but they don't want to pay for what might not happen. Banks finance based on history, as long as the projections look the same or better.

- *I deserve something for my sweat equity.* I had a client whose business had erratic profits. She once said, "There's value in that I've been around for 15 years." Answer: yes, there is, if it shows up on the bottom line. The more profits, the higher the value.

- *It's worth a multiple of revenue.* If two businesses are in the same industry, have similar sales, one has 15% profit and the other 2% profit, are they worth the same (all other things being equal)?

- *Rules of thumb are reliable.* If 100 businesses sell for 4X earnings and 100 sell for 3X earnings the rule of thumb says they all sell for an average of 3.5X. I've had buyers insist they won't pay more than the average, even when the business has much higher profits than average.

Creative Financing is Not Financial Hocus Pocus, but...

In the first edition of my book *Buying a Business That Makes You Rich*, I had a section of 27 creative financing techniques. In the second edition I removed that section, mentioned a few ideas, and said that, for a deal in the size range of an SBA loan (up to about $7 million in transaction value) there's rarely a need for most creative finance techniques.

That said, many things can still be done for larger deals. Creative finance is not financial hocus-pocus or wishful thinking. It's using the assets or cash flow of the business to help pay for the business or pay back the buyer, with an emphasis these days on the latter. (Also realize that this chapter is more for a buyer than a seller.)

Let's look at some of the things you can't or probably don't want to do when you have an SBA loan:

- *Assume debt.* A no-no with an SBA loan.

- *A buyer can't buy cash.* Unless it's to cover deferred revenue or deposit.

- *An earnout.* At least not a "positive" earnout, as in, "I'll pay more if the business grows." You can do a claw-back or negative earnout if the maximum price meets debt coverage ratios from day one, as if it's being paid from day one.

- *Seasonal payments.* You can have variable payments based on seasonality on a seller note, but is it worth it if that note is only 10% or so of the price. Many years ago, a client bought a very seasonal business. Six months of boom, six months of blah. The seller financed the deal and payment schedule matched the seasonality.

Now for what you can still do (and should look to do):

- *Manage the inventory better, and turn stuff on shelves into cash.* A client bought a company whose seller loved seeing full racks of inventory. The buyer managed inventory better, and in the first year he turned over $200,000 of it into cash, repaying part of his down payment.

- *Don't buy outdated inventory.* Reduce the price accordingly, the seller should keep it, and sell it any way he can, even to the buyer if ever needed.

- *Sell assets and lease them.* A good example of this is when a buyer sells a fleet of vehicles and leases new ones.

- *Hire the seller as an employee or a consultant.* Make the payments part of the purchase price, but be careful of SBA rules about the seller staying on.

- *Sell shares to management, post-close.* This works a lot better if management pays in cash, versus the buyer taking a note.

I use the example of Ockham's Razor in Chapter 44, "The Magic Question," and it applies here as well: the simplest solution is often the best. Don't overcomplicate things if you don't have to. If the deal can be done with cash from the buyer, a bank loan, and a small seller note, then take the easy road and get it done.

None of the books or webinars on buying a business with no cash (or very little cash) are applicable to mature, profitable, fairly priced businesses. They may apply to distressed companies, and the best buyer for those is a firm in the same industry. In the COVID-19 world, I'm hearing of companies selling for nothing more than the assumption of debt, and these are obviously not profitable businesses.

Chapter 51

A Story Showing How Mergers Created Big Profits

By Ted Leverette, Founder, "Partner" On-Call Network LLC

It shows the power of economies of scale. Of eliminating competition without hurting anyone. Employees remained employed. The sellers of their companies got a fair deal. Customers got more and better service. My client, the owner/buyer, made lots of money.

It's also a cautionary tale.

It's a little idea with the potential for big opportunity. Especially if you get the timing right. My idea: If you can't beat 'em, join 'em!

You might recall the proliferation, in the 1980s and early 1990s, of print-shop franchises. They created more print shops than the marketplace could profitably support. (You're seeing this kind of unhelpful proliferation and industry saturation, today, for other kinds of businesses, aren't you?)

The owner of an independently owned and operated shop hired me. He was nervous because the customer-pie wasn't growing. Worse, the slices were diminishing, thanks to new competition generated by the incursion of franchised print-shop startups. The owner was thinking about selling his profitable company. I suggested he postpone selling until we could improve the company's competitive advantages, which would increase the value of the business.

Using a script, which I prepared and rehearsed with him, the owner asked competing print shops if they were worried about industry saturation. Most were.

So he bought two of them, each of which served mostly differing market segments within his locale—the kinds of customers he did not serve. Both of the acquisitions were earning a modest profit. Their owners wanted out because they, too, didn't want to cope with what was looking to be profit-weakening industry saturation.

The idea was to operate from one location, so the surviving company (my client's) could be more efficient and profitable.

Before the consolidation, these print shops were running only one shift. So the soon-to-be-larger company shut down the shop with the least desirable location. The employees from the closed shop went to work for the surviving shop. They worked the (new) second shift.

Later, in the next M&A transaction, the acquired company was shut down, and its employees were hired for the (new) third shift at the surviving shop. (There was no second or third shift before the consolidation.)

Closing two print shops enabled the surviving company to sell most of the tangible assets that were owned by his former competitors. The proceeds from the sale of equipment and vehicles, plus the elimination of redundant inventory and overhead, created a windfall profit for the surviving print shop.

And each time we merged a print shop, we cut out one competitor.

My client used some of the cash he had generated from selling surplus equipment, in addition to the cost savings by elimination of overhead (rent and lots of other expenses), to pay down the financing he had incurred to acquire the competitors.

The company immediately increased its profit and improved its competitive advantages. And then the owner sold it for a lot more money than he would have received had he sold the company before doing what we did.

You can use this technique to grow your business, even if your industry is not saturated with competitors. But think twice before trying to grow by consolidating businesses within a (soon-to-be) suffering industry.

The accomplishments achieved in the printing industry were significantly reduced when desktop computers, printers and software made it easy and cheap for former customers of print shops to design and publish documents. (And with 3D printing, which is coming on strong right now, it won't be long before other kinds of companies lose market share.)

Timing and target selection are key.
Ted Leverette "Partner" On-Call Network
tedjleverette@partneroncall.com

Chapter 52

The Importance of Confidentiality and Valuation in the Sale of a Business

By Curt Case, Managing Director, ACT Capital Advisors

One of the most critical things for a business owner, considering the sale of a business, is to have a sound idea of the business's value range in the marketplace. It is also very desirable for an owner to know how to maximize value within that range.

A privately-owned business is quite often its owner's principal asset, and it usually represents years, if not decades, of hard work. Anyone who has done it knows full well just how difficult building and operating a successful business can be. Many challenges had to be met, and many sacrifices had to be made along the way.

Selling a privately-owned business presents a whole new set challenges no less difficult to overcome. Experience shows that each company represents a new and unique set of circumstances, problems and opportunities. Marketing the company, selecting the best buyer, and constructively negotiating sales agreements is more difficult than most owners would anticipate.

With some exceptions, it is a rare entrepreneur that starts a business with the express purpose of selling it. If one did, most decisions would be guided by the goal of preparing the business for sale. Consideration and priorities such as new product development, accelerated growth, investments in in employee training, increasing market share, and minimizing taxes are typical business objectives. These objectives, however, may well be inconsistent with maximizing a business's value.

Adding to the challenges facing an owner is the need to continue to run the business. Another important consideration is that, in most cases, it is critical that employees, customers, suppliers and competitors do not know that the business is for sale.

Several cautions to assure that a business is not sold for less than full value (and, indeed, to sell for maximum value) are noted here:

- Maintain confidentiality.

- Do not overexpose the business.

- Have a clear, defensible analysis and value expectation to present to buyer(s).

- Don't rely on "standard formulas," friends or associates to value estimates.

- Do *not* offer the business for a stated value.

- Properly state the true earnings power of the business with properly "recast" financial statements.

- Avoid selling to a competitor or a "walk in" offer without adequately testing the market and employing competition among buyers as a value enhancer.

- Where appropriate, sell the future rather than the past.

Curt Case
ACT Capital Advisors
ccase@actcapitaladvisors.com

Chapter 53

A 'Win-Win' Negotiation Starts with Business Pricing

By Gregory Kovsky, President,
International Business Associates

The deal element with the greatest potential for confrontation between buyer and seller in a transaction involving a business sale is the price. The value of a business can be established within a narrow range, approximately 10%, by a party with an appropriate level of knowledge, experience, and professional skill. If a business is brought to market at a "fair" market value, that negotiation of this element will be mitigated.

In a business sale transaction, once the parties have agreed on the price—an issue in which the seller has a vested interest in getting the highest value possible and the buyer has a vested interest in completing the acquisition at the lowest value possible—then, judging from my experience as an intermediary who has facilitated over 300 "win-win" transactions, the parties are no longer on adversarial footings, but working collaboratively to achieve a common goal.

If a business is brought to market at a value out of alignment with the market, then negotiations will be longer and will likely result in a higher emotional and mental burden on the parties, if agreement can be reached. These increased negotiations have the potential to negatively color perspective of the other party. A negative view of the other party is a poor foundation to build a relationship between buyer and seller.

The accuracy of the business value of a company for sale will traditionally be determined by a three-tiered, buyer-side vetting process. The first level of analysis of the price will be performed by the party interested in the potential acquisition. This party is the most open for consideration of the market value offered, because they are mentally and emotionally engaged to complete the acquisition. Failure to convince the potential business buyer to "buy in" at a value in the neighborhood of the asking price will result in the death of a deal. A seller has only one opportunity to make a first impression. So a business should be brought to market with price and terms reflective of the reality of market conditions.

Assuming that the buyer engages and wishes to purchase the business, the asking price will likely be next evaluated by the party's CPA or CFO. This professional will not bring emotion into the assessment; the assessment will be purely analytical. A "thumbs down" on the deal by an accounting professional has a high probability of being a deal-killer.

An acquisition endorsed at the first two levels has a significant third hurdle to clear. That third hurdle is the bank or investors supporting the acquisition. Banks and investors are by nature conservative, reluctant to provide capital unless a high probability of proper debt coverage ratios and/or a return on investment exists. A negative assessment of the deal at this level will result in either a need to change transaction terms or buyer withdrawal.

An experienced, professional intermediary should know how a buyer, the buyer's CPA, and the bank will assess value before a business is priced. If that has occurred, the probability of proper pricing and a completed "win-win" transaction is enhanced.

Gregory Kovsky
www.ibainc.com
(425) 454-3052
gregory@ibainc.com

Negotiation—It's Not Table Pounding

In my first real job after college, I was involved with some union negotiations. This was not the most pleasurable thing to do, and I constantly reminded myself that most buy-sell negotiations are pretty tame compared to union negotiations, and the parties have to remain friends, or the deal will die.

There is usually give-and-take, except when one party is smitten with the other (buyer or seller fever). So what really gets negotiated? Price often comes first, and terms follow. If a bank is involved, the bank must approve the payment parameters, so both sides must understand the bank conditions.

Some common negotiated items include:

- **Working capital.** How much is needed? How is it calculated? If inventory is involved, is it usable and salable? Banks love it when the deal includes adequate working capital. (See Chapter 46, "Working Capital Adjuster," for more information on working capital and the working capital adjuster formula.)

- **Work in process.** This should be on the balance sheet as a current asset for costs in excess of billings and a current liability for deposits. You may think that would make it simple, but it doesn't always. On one recent deal, we agreed that the seller would make the margin on the amount of deposits and the buyer would do so on the remainder of the billing.

- **Seller note.** A seller note is the seller's "skin in the game," which banks and buyers usually want.

- **Earnout.** An earnout is a condition in which part of the price, or the additional price, is contingent on future performance. Sellers, your CPA and attorney will scream when they hear of an earnout, and they will tell you that you will never see one dollar of it. That is an overreaction, especially if there is a good reason for an earnout, though litigators will jump for joy at such news.

Good reasons for an earnout include:

- The seller has a new product line that hasn't been exploited yet.

- The firm has huge dependencies, e.g., extremely high customer concentration or product domination.

- One employee has too much responsibility.

Bad reasons for an earnout include:

- The seller wants more than the business is worth.

- The buyer wants to pay the fair market price only if the business grows (transferring risk to the seller).

- Also, earnouts are not allowed if an SBA loan is involved, but claw backs are allowed.

Three final tips:

- You have to stay friendly with the other party, as you'll be working together for months or longer.

- Never let the attorneys get involved with negotiations on business issues. This is a deal-killer.

- Trust your team, and use them to keep your emotions in check.

There will also be legal negotiations, and that's between the lawyers. One issue that always comes up is the subject of "knowledge qualifiers." The buyer's attorney will want the seller to represent and warranty what they know about the business, and which they provide in writing as schedules to the purchase-and-sale agreement. The seller's attorney will want to say, "To the best of seller's knowledge" they represent and warranty.

My opinion is that the owner of a business should know all about its day-to-day operations if active in the business. An owner who is in a nursing home may not know all about them. I did have a client selling to his operations manager who had been running the business for a few years. It was easy to say that the seller didn't have knowledge of the day-to-day, but this is the exception, not the norm.

Chapter 55

Realize It's Complex

A friend called regarding a client of his who was thinking of selling to his COO/GM. The holidays got in the way, and then he told me he felt they didn't have a good understanding of what it takes to do a deal. So I provided them with a redacted PSA. It caused them to pause and think.

Business sellers often underestimate the complexity of what's involved in selling a company. It's their cute little puppy, so they think everybody will think it's adorable. Even if others find it adorable, there's still a lot of work to do. The amount of detailed information requested by the buyer, bank and attorneys can be overwhelming. Deal fatigue is common.

One of my common sayings is, "Just when the seller thinks they've been asked every possible question, the bank asks more." Furthermore, buyers will ask the same question more than once, which can annoy sellers, or even lead them to believe the buyer isn't listening. I coach sellers to expect this for two reasons:

1. Buyers are taking a drink from a firehose, and some of the information sprays away from them.

2. They'll ask the same question again to see if they get the same answer.

All of this is before the aforementioned PSA. In fact, the letter of intent (aka offer) is often filled with legalese that businesspeople aren't familiar with. Some tips for sellers:

- Your job is to run the company, and the LOI will probably say you agree to run it the same way you always have. So bring in a trusted employee or two (or more) to handle the information-gathering. Make sure the employees sign an NDA, and consider giving them a bonus upon closing, or a retention bonus if they stay with the buyer for (let's say) one year.

- Get to know the buyer as a person. This will make the sale a much smoother process.

- Understand that you will sign an agreement saying you represent and warranty everything in the contract. So pay close attention to all the transmitted information.

- Realize that whatever you verbally tell a buyer is treated (almost) as hearsay. You will be asked to provide backup, in writing, for just about everything to do with the company, so don't be surprised. All of this written information is part of the PSA in the form of schedules. A quick story: a CPA once called me and asked, "Why do we have to provide all of this information about the customers? We already told the buyer all of this." The answer is obvious: to prove that what you said is true and correct.

Most businesspeople are optimistic. It's a necessary trait, and sellers are no different. The complexity of a buy-sell deal can be extremely high and reduce optimism. It's usually nothing like what you've done before.

The process of buying a company can take at least a year. Selling a company can take 6-12 months. A lot of moving parts are involved, so figure if buyer and seller meet today, it will probably be 120 days before they close, as relationship building, information gathering, analysis, deal structure and negotiation of it, financing, due diligence, and legal are all to follow. Some but not all of these steps are taken concurrently. Most buyers will not engage their attorney until they are assured of bank financing.

Chapter 56

It's Open Kimono Time

For sellers, this is your scariest dream (nightmare), and also your time to shine. It's tough to bare your business soul, even to a qualified buyer who you think is a perfect fit, and who has a signed Letter of Intent (LOI).

But you have to do it. The buyer gets to see everything. Absolutely everything. What's included in "everything?" The following, and anything else needed to get financing and close the deal:

- Tax returns for three to five years

- Financial statements for three to five years

- Monthly financial statements for the last couple of years and the current year to date

- AR and AP aging

- Asset lists

- Employee information, agreements, and eventually key employee and management team interviews

- Customer list and customer interviews (disguised so not to reveal the sale)

- Vendor scrutiny

- Your lease

- Undisclosed liabilities, which are often leases, contracts (advertising or equipment), and paid time off (as many small businesses don't put PTO on the balance sheet)

- Environmental reports

- All legal matters, including litigation, noncompliance with regulations, etc.

The buyer's attorney will have a due-diligence list and it will probably correspond to the list of exhibits and schedules to the PSA. This makes it easy when it comes time to finalize the agreement.

Remember, this is what you are representing and warrantying as true and correct. For example, if one section asks about vendor or customer contracts and there are none, you write, "Not applicable, no written agreements, simply a month-to-month arrangement." Then, if after closing the top vendor drops your buyer as a customer, the buyer has no recourse to you, as you disclosed there was no long-term agreement, so she had full knowledge of the situation.

What's important is when things are disclosed. Customers and vendors are usually not contacted until the financial due diligence is done and the buyer signs off on it as completed. Employees are often not introduced to the buyer until all other due diligence is completed and the PSA is signed, with a contingency for meeting the employees and final funding.

I mentioned that it's your time to shine. Buyers get angst when the seller is slow on providing diligence information. Their skeptical brain starts working overtime, wondering what's wrong, what's being covered up, etc. You remove that angst by showing all requested documents and figures, plus unrequested ones that you feel will benefit the buyer.

For buyers, you also have to disclose everything about yourself to the seller, although your list is a lot shorter. You're representing who you say you are and providing and representing your personal financial statement if the seller is financing part of the deal. If a bank is involved, they'll get every piece of information about you that they can, and may well ask for more.

Where a Buyer Should Start Due Diligence: Customers

Rule #1 for B2B companies: If the seller won't let you talk to the customers as either a reference check or as a customer satisfaction survey, put the deal on hold or kill it.

Rule #2: See Rule #1.

In 25 years, I've had only three or four issues with customer diligence. Maybe I'm so adamant about Rule #1 because of a buyer client in 2005. This was an industry with a large upfront expenditure for equipment, followed by service and upgrades. When it came time to reach out to customers, the seller told the buyer he couldn't talk to them, I couldn't talk to them, nobody could talk to them. The reason given was that the industry was so tight, so competitive, that word would get out and create problems.

I told him to put the deal on hold. The attorney told him to kill the deal, and he told us he understood the reasoning and trusted the seller (she was smooth). It turned out that the top customer, who brought in 25% of the company sales, was doing a "test kitchen" of competitors' products and didn't invite the current supplier to participate. The customer hated the supplier so much for nickel-and-diming them over the years that the customer didn't want anything to do with that supplier—and the seller knew it.

But there's more to customer diligence than disguised calling. Here are some other aspects of customer due diligence (and they're important, because the majority of the company's value comes from customer-driven intangibles, i.e., goodwill):

- **Diversity—aka customer concentration issues.** In the SMB market, our first benchmark occurs when any customers are more than 10% of sales, especially when it's the same customer every year. We also realize that most B2B companies have some concentration, and that's when the other factors come into play. Now, start getting up to 20-25% with one customer or over half of sales to three customers, and there's a potential problem. A big problem.

- **Who are the customers?** Are they large firms that could change buying policies overnight? If they are small businesses, are they stable? What are their ownership statuses and succession plans?

- **How loyal are the customers?** This really means, does the company provide value on quality and service? I was talking to an owner recently who said they have customers who will switch suppliers for 10¢ a unit. He doesn't chase them (to get them back), because it's not worth the hassle or cost.

- **Pricing.** Are different customers getting different prices, meaning higher or lower margins to the business? Losing a customer with low prices may be a blessing in disguise (as they're often the most difficult).

- **Growth.** Are your customers growing? Can you grow with them without ruining your diversity? Can you keep up with their needs, or are you close to capacity?

Businesses, small businesses especially, are really the people: employees and customers.

Chapter 58

Mutual Understanding Fuels Due Diligence

By Michelle Bomberger, CEO and Managing Attorney at Equinox Business Law Group PLLC

Without question, due diligence is one of the most critical and challenging parts of a transaction. On the surface, it appears to be an exchange of documents and information about the business being purchased. However, the success of due diligence rides on the trust between the buyer and the seller. Both buyers and sellers need to prepare for due diligence with the other party's mindset in focus. The seller is coming into due diligence with a lot of confidence in their business—they know it inside and out. On the other hand, the buyer is coming into due diligence with little to no information—they know that they need to ask the right questions. When each party's due diligence focus is solely on their own needs, the trust that has developed can crumble and jeopardize the transaction.

Because the buyer needs to cover all bases, their due diligence request is broad-based with many document requests. The seller invests time and money in getting the documents organized, and they are ready to share all information gathered. The buyer is pleased to receive the organized information provided by the seller, but often some requested information is omitted. Missing information raises additional questions from the buyer or their advisors, and the buyer requests additional information.

This process is iterative and can go on for months in a deal. Understandably, each party's frustration mounts. The seller is frustrated because they've already disclosed "everything," but more so because they are confident that the business is in good shape with no skeletons in the closet. The buyer is frustrated because they feel that their questions are reasonable and that the seller should be able and willing to answer them easily.

This frustration breaks down the trust built during initial negotiations. The seller can't believe the buyer doesn't trust that all is in order with the business, nor can the buyer believe that the seller can't or won't provide the information requested. The reality is that the process is emotionally taxing for both parties. Yes, it appears to be just an exchange of documents and information. But after the first round of due diligence, it becomes something more. The investment level of each party has increased, and the additional questioning feels more personal. If this interaction is not managed well, the deal may suffer.

Each party must enter the due diligence process with eyes open to the process and the other party's expectations and emotions. They should ask their advisors what to expect from the process and how to keep the transaction on track. They should encourage advisors to focus on what's important to *this* deal, not simply take a broadbrush approach to cover all potential risks. It's crucial to balance these considerations.

Due diligence is emotional and time-consuming for both sides. By understanding the other party's mindset and efforts, you can set expectations to smooth the way and manage a successful process and relationship.

Michelle Bomberger
Equinox Business Law
michelle@equinoxbusinesslaw.com

Chapter 59

Transition Plan

The most overlooked part of the process is the transition plan. During negotiations, it's often an annoying detail with such boilerplate language as, "Seller will provide up to 30 hours a week of support for 90 days," just to get the LOI signed. Even when the language becomes more detailed when defining in-person time, phone time, email time, etc., very seldom is there a discussion of exactly what the buyer needs in the way of transition support.

Warning: Not having a transition plan can disrupt the company post-close, waste time, and possibly even derail the deal.

What both buyer and seller don't want to have happen is what occurred a number of years ago when both buyer and seller ignored advice and paid zero attention to the transition plan. As I understand it, they got together the day after closing, the buyer asked the seller to tell him what he needed to know about the business, and the seller replied, "What do you want to know?" This went on a few times until the buyer called me and the seller called one of his advisors.

My advice to the buyer was to sit down with the seller, use the template I had provided him, and work out a plan for what he needed to learn and when he needed to learn it. It took a while, but they got it done.

Each of my other books contains a detailed template for a transition plan, put together by a very anal-retentive client. If you would like a copy, please email me at john@johnmartinka.com. For now, I will give you an outline of the plan's major points, from the buyer's perspective:

- **Before closing:** Write the business plan and budget, have your legal entity established, and take care of all annoying little details (email me for a checklist on this). Ask the seller for the five most important things you'll need to learn, and keep going from there.

- **First month:** Get to know the people, shadow the seller, explore growth opportunities, and really think about how long you want the seller around. Work with the seller on meeting customers.

- **Second month:** Have the seller take off for a week so the employees realize the buyer is the new boss. Learn more about the customers, vendors, employee capabilities and company culture, and determine your best use over the next six months.

- **Third month:** By now you will probably be phasing the seller out and getting in deep into what you want to change, so you should have a really good understanding of the business.

One of the best tactics to gain this understanding is to survey the employees, at least the management team. They usually have great ideas and insights and often have been held back by an owner comfortable with where the business is, revenue- and profit-wise. Funny story: one buyer surveyed the employees of the newly acquired business, and one question asked was, "What is the business' biggest weakness?" The answers from all management team members were similar to, as one of them wrote it, "The biggest weakness just walked out the door."

There's a lot for the seller to teach and a lot for the buyer to learn. It's all about the intricacies of the business, not general business. Concentrate on the people:

- **the employees,** who are scared and wondering about job security;

- **the customers,** and building a relationship with them, especially the top ones;

- **the suppliers,** to assure them of your capabilities so they're not worried about getting paid.

Chapter 60

Closing, Here We Come

Whether you're a buyer or a seller, this is the moment you've been waiting for, right? It's the big day, and the start of your next great adventure in life. For sellers, it's a sizable chunk of money in your bank account. For buyers, it's a chance to make your ideas come to fruition, not to mention all the debt you now have.

Sometimes all final documents are signed in a formal ceremony in a lawyer's office or the escrow attorney's office. Other times they are signed separately, scanned, and e-mailed to the closing attorney. When signed at the actual closing, there are rarely contingencies. As of the time of this writing, most if not all banks require an independent attorney/agent to handle the closing.

Other times, the final papers are signed a week or two before closing, with contingencies for the buyer meeting the employees, customers or vendors. Meeting the employees is the most common contingency, and unless the employees walk out en masse, the deal is on. (It's never been an issue in my deals.)

The closing attorney, often an independent escrow person, will prepare a statement for both buyer and seller. The buyer is told how much money to wire to the escrow account and this be for the down payment, costs for such items as lien checks, taxes due, escrow fee, and so on. The seller's statement will show the gross funds he will receive and will also show deductions for costs, which may include an intermediary commission, an escrow fee, and the like.

The money from the buyer and the bank goes into escrow, and the buyer and seller will sign "escrow instructions" to the escrow agent, which will determine when the money will be wired to the seller. There may be no contingencies, and the money will be wired once all funds have cleared into the account. It may require the buyer waiving contingencies, as mentioned above, clearance of liens, bank approval that all debts are paid, or something else.

But before you get to closing, there's a lot the buyer must do. The following is from a document I give buyers as a checklist of things to do before closing. This list was compiled from input I received from 8-10 buyers who had closed on deals in the two years prior to when I asked them. A lot of these items are the nagging, little administrivia things that drive many people nuts, but they must be done. Sellers, you will be involved in a lot of this.

Determine legal structure[1]

- Sole proprietor

- Partnership

- Corporation: C or S

- LLC

Administration Matters

Government

- Federal and state registrations

- County and city regulations

- Pick your business name and register it

- State and local business licenses

- U.S. Department of Revenue

- Employer identification number (EIN)

- S Corporation election and filing

- Hazardous materials (hazmat) reports[2]

- Local permits and licensing[2]

- Confirmation of seller's existing corporation or LLC existence

- Registered agents address

- Forms: All tax forms, labor and industries (L&I), sales, unemployment, personal property, etc.

- If an asset purchase is involved, dissolve seller's entity or have him/her relinquish the trade name to you

Non-Government

- Bank: deposits, credit card processing, lines of credit, etc.

- Telephone: long distance, local, cell

- Utilities

- Internet, website, shippers (FedEx, UPS)

- Copyrights, trademarks, and other intellectual property, including trade name registration

- Insurance: property, liability, vehicle, life (bank may require), health, disability, etc.

- New business cards, stationery

- Lease

- Software licenses, passwords, etc.

- Off-balance sheet items: equipment leases, advertising contracts, etc.

- Employment agreements/non-compete agreements, W-9s & W-4s

- Contracts with vendors, customers, etc.

- Vendor and customer lists, including *all* contact information

- Signage, printing, labels, etc.

- Change vehicle registrations

Financial

- Books and records: What system, who does it, does your CPA approve of it, etc.

- Vendor list: Must you apply for credit?[3]

- Closing reports, liens, taxes due, etc.[4]

- Pro-rated expenses and revenues, including accounting for customer deposits for future work and the cash needed to fulfill such work

- Post-closing settlement date

- Life insurance: This is a timely issue. Your bank will require it, and your seller note may do so. It can take 6-8 weeks to get a policy issued, so you must start early.

1. Your attorney can guide you through this process. Make sure you check with your CPA to make sure your chosen entity type is the best for anticipated tax issues.

2. For these issues and others, make sure you have the seller fill out the Initial Disclosure Form (mentioned in Chapter 20).

3. To get an accurate list of all vendors, get a list of the AP aging (even if you're not getting the AP as part of the deal).

4. Whoever closes your deal should handle all details such as taxes due, forms due, lien filings and removals, etc.

Disclaimer: The above is not a due-diligence form or checklist. It supplements the buyer's due-diligence forms. It is designed as a guide for the little things it takes to prepare for closing, get your entity off the ground, and assure a smooth transition. It is not guaranteed to be all-inclusive, as all deals and situations are different. Items are not listed in any particular order.

Chapter 61

19 reasons you should consider growing by acquisition

This last chapter is longer because growing by acquisition is such an important strategy, especially in the COVID-19 and post-COVID-19 world. For companies whose owners fear the pain of rebuilding (again), selling to another firm may be the best option to get the highest price (and maybe even a job).

The cake: 16 solid reasons (in alphabetical order)

1. Acquire great talent, including the seller
2. Assets are cheaper as a package
3. Competitive advantages: Exploit them
4. Dependencies reduced
5. Diamonds in the rough
6. Diversify your product offerings
7. Easy money is the best kind
8. Integration is easier
9. Location, location, location
10. Make a competitor go away
11. Psychology—be part of a winning team
12. Risk—it's a lot lower
13. Overhead the same, volume higher
14. Synergy
15. Technologies
16. Vendor relationship strategies

The icing—the top three

17. Customers (efficiency vs. make more calls)

18. Yes, we can!

19. The bigger you are…the better

1. Acquire great talent, including the seller

Good employees are hard to find and are often not in the job market. Just talk to any executive recruiter. While all buyers want capable employees, most strategic buyers (that's you) also prefer to see a solid management team in place.

Great employees with industry knowledge and experience are in the job market even less. When you are looking for great salespeople, they won't change if they've already got a good thing going. Here are some statistics from an executive recruiter, which explains why it's tough to find good people.

- 82% of people aren't searching for a job.

- Leadership, or lack thereof, is the top reason why management people switch jobs (not money).

- 46% of millennials left their last job because of its lack of career growth potential.

If you acquire their company and create an atmosphere of growth, those employees will want to stay. While I can't comment on the culture in all companies, I do know that many small family-owned businesses have owners who are coasting. They are doing very well, they aren't working too hard, and they don't want to disrupt the nice moneymaking system they have.

One of my clients had trouble keeping a licensed person (in this case, an electrician with an administrator's license). His strategy was to acquire a small electrical contractor to head up his new electrical department. The story we painted was incredible, especially for an owner sick and tired of all of the admin work that accompanies running a very small business.

The picture of the advantages included taking over all the administration (all financial aspects, scheduling, purchasing, and more), the ability to grow a division and mentor people, and a full benefits package including vacation, medical insurance, 401k match, steady income, etc.

Again, if you can't hire them, it may make sense to buy them.

The employees may be younger and have more energy and ideas on how to grow and challenge themselves and the firm. To the owner, this could mean a bigger payday, but with the corresponding risk of slightly lower profits if the ideas don't work, or a temporary profit reduction if an investment is made in the new idea. In addition, the owner's skills have often been maxed out, to the point that they just can't grow the business anymore.

Maybe you keep the owner on the team. You buy the business and keep his wealth of product and customer knowledge on the team. You get productivity, and the seller is happy to be rid of the management responsibilities.

Warning: Some sellers can't accept working for someone else after years of being in charge.

I once had two clients (coincidentally, both in Los Angeles and both distributors) who hired me to find companies in their specific industries. The prime motivator for both was to acquire great salespeople. They needed people with industry knowledge and experience but were having trouble finding people who were willing to change jobs. Buying another company with a good sales staff made more sense than trying to steal employees.

2.   Assets are cheaper as a package

Tangible assets are a sunk cost. Once you have them—be they vehicles, machines, forklifts, or space—you have the cost or payments.

You need to make them efficient. All businesses struggle with this for tangible and human assets.

At some point you have to buy a new machine (or hire a new person), because you're over capacity on current equipment, people are working too much overtime, or some other reason. However, once you buy that piece of equipment, your capacity increases and your utilization drops, so you have to generate more sales to run the equipment at a profitable rate.

Wouldn't it be nice if the equipment, just like people, came with sales orders? Of course it would. And that's why buying another company can be a good way to get needed equipment with corresponding customers. As the header for this section states, these assets can be cheaper as a package (versus buying new or used assets that don't come with customers).

As emphasized in the previous section, you also get the employees who know how to operate the equipment (or provide the service). As I write this, there's a shortage of qualified people in the marketplace. I don't care if it's machinists, salespeople, line workers, or something else. Owners have told me they can't find qualified people who can pass a background check or a drug test. An acquisition just might be the answer to this problem.

3.   Competitive advantages: Exploit them

My friend Tim Riley created an industry when he started his company, Door-to-Door Storage, in the late 1990s. Tim came out of Shurgard Storage, had the idea of mobile storage (deliver a pod, load it, return it to a controlled-climate warehouse), raised angel and venture capital financing, and gave birth to an idea.

But the competitive advantage he had was low, as were the barriers of entry. It wasn't long after he launched his business when I met a person doing the same thing with a different name. Now it's a saturated industry; almost every moving, warehouse, and rental company (like U-Haul) offers similar services.

Contrast the above with these examples:

- An environmental engineering firm that has built a reputation of doing great work, on time, and at a fair price. They are the "go to" firm in their market with many, many law firms (environmental attorneys).

- A software company whose product "fixes" the gaps in major server software programs.

- The machine shop with its own proprietary product that does what no other product does for its aerospace customers.

- The outsource HR service company that keeps small businesses compliant with all moving-target rules and regulations at one-third to one-half the cost of the full-time employees they replaced.

What is your target and your competitive advantage? Be it quality, value, service, intellectual property, or something else, this is your opportunity to combine forces and exploit them.

4.   Dependencies reduced

Dependencies are a huge issue in most small businesses. By being larger, you can reduce most or all of the following:

1.   Customers
2.   Employees
3.   Management abilities
4.   Product
5.   Owner

Not too much explanation is needed here. You will yield more customers over your expanded revenue base, more employees, deeper management, less product concentration, and most of all, more talent to take a load off the owner. And an owner dependency is often the brightest red flag for most profitable small businesses. Of course, the owner must be willing to take advantage of the deeper bench by delegating to them.

5.   Diamonds in the rough

This may mean buy a losing or struggling business that yields personal income to the owner but no real profit. Or it could mean buying a business where you can see things that can be done to make it more than it is now.

Often the mediocre business has no options other than to struggle along, close the doors, or sell to another business. Rarely will individuals or other financial buyers (those needing an income from the business) buy a loser. That means their options are very limited, as only a small percentage of companies ever consider growth by acquisition, which makes it an even stronger strategy for those who do.

This can be a good find at a low cost, perhaps even on an earnout basis, where payments are made to the seller based on sales or profits or the increase of sales and profits, and are not guaranteed. And these can still be win-win deals. You get volume, people, and more, and the seller gets more money for the company that she wouldn't otherwise have received, or gets some money she wouldn't have received in another situation.

Technology can often produce large-profit growth, even for non-tech businesses. A service business with burned-out owners (actually, they were well beyond burned out—they were fried) had a website that acted like a brochure. To order services, the customers had to call in, and we all know how that works—repeated phone-tag.

Even if an order is left on voicemail, it must be confirmed. In any event, it takes an employee to process the order, and the customer must take the time to make the calls, return calls, and talk about the order. The buyer noticed this during analysis and within two months had an online ordering system. It saved the customers time and hassle, and it increased his staff's productivity a lot. It's not rocket science; it's observing and looking at things through the customers' eyes, and creating a "diamond in the rough."

In any event, as an ongoing business the pool of targets is larger than if you are someone buying a first business (as most individual buyers avoid troubled companies like they avoid a toothache, because both are a pain). Look at the other 18 reasons for growth by acquisition, and use this reason to leverage your efforts.

6.   Diversify your product offerings

Almost every salesperson has left a client's business thinking, "If only we had the X and Y product line, I could sell it to him, save him money, and make more myself." Of course it's tough to get those product lines, especially if you're starting from zero with the supplier.

Fred's company is an environmental testing laboratory. We came to find out that the industry contains different types of labs, and his original company dealt primarily with contaminants (ground water, soil, etc.), so I like to call this a "dirty lab." Another type of lab, as in his second acquisition, is what I call a "clean lab," testing drinking water (wells, reservoirs, municipal systems, etc.).

We also learned that it is tough—in fact, darn near impossible—to do clean testing in a dirty lab, as the contaminants get in the air. Now he has a clean lab and a dirty lab. He can offer each lab's customer base more services than before. That's synergy.

The same applies to companies with a product. So why not buy a firm with complementary product lines and diversify what your people can sell? It doesn't have to be a huge company. It can be a small company that will have full support of its vendor because you can plug the products into your customer base for almost instantaneous growth (of the new product lines).

The products don't have to be similar; the customer bases merely have to use both types of products to leverage this idea. I remember one owner who sold packaging materials (boxes). He believed he could acquire a company that sold any kind of supplies to warehouses. What else do warehouses use? Paper, tape, janitorial supplies, racks, material handling equipment, and more. Don't limit yourself. Think creatively.

7.   Easy money is the best kind

How much does it cost to add a new product? To expand into a new market? To hire salespeople to generate new customers?

It can be a lot of money, and where do you get all that money? Will the bank lend you money to do these things? If so, how much, and on what terms and conditions?

You'll get all the money for organic growth by saving your profits and/or taking out a conventional bank loan, but money for an acquisition is usually much easier to find. As we'll see in more detail later, banks really like acquisition loans. The bottom line is, if you tell your banker you're going to grow by 50% or more in the next year and need a loan for the growth, I'm guessing you'll be politely shown the door. At the very least you'll be asked for detailed projections, an analysis showing the chances of success, and intense scrutiny.

Now imagine you show them the profit-and-loss statement and the tax return for your target company, with more than enough historical annual flow to make the payments. A short synopsis of why the target is a fit, a brief overview of the integration plan, and a combined organizational chart may be everything else you'll need (and you'll need these anyway to make an acquisition). This is easy money, compared to just about any other type of growth funding.

8.   Integration is easier

"People don't like change" is an old expression. What many people really don't like is having their routines changed, especially without a reason or reward. Yes, there will be some change, and it will take time, but it's often easier than finding talent, integrating individuals and changing the culture. There are four components to this:

A. A breath of fresh air

The sales manager at a recently acquired firm thanked me for getting the deal done and said the new buyer was a "breath of fresh air." The new owner, unlike the seller, listened to the employees' ideas and let them act on their ideas, and he was willing to take risks. Too often employees get in a rut. They like the company and their jobs, but it gets to be routine. When the boss ignores them, they lose enthusiasm and leave.

You can inject a breath of fresh air by buying another business. Enthusiasm is hard to teach, and it's contagious. The excitement of an acquisition can fire up your team and the team of the acquired business with a new and rewarding challenge. Often their company is being sold because the owner is retiring or burned out. In either event, that owner has probably been coasting while the employees are constantly having new ideas. Put two fired-up teams together and let them use their abilities, and you have 2+2=22.

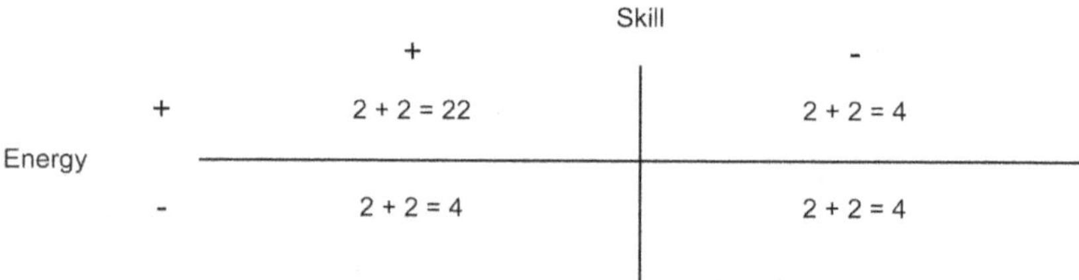

B. A management team

You should assemble a larger management team, whether it comprises senior or junior people. This should give you a more diverse skill set, or the ability to replace duplicate people with other skill sets. Finally, there will be new ideas from their people regarding your operation and from your people regarding theirs.

C. Friendliness

The first assumption here is that a win-win deal is structured. What you are offering to the seller is true value, be it a successful retirement, salvation of their sinking ship, or a rescue from a catastrophic event (divorce, death, disability).

When it's a win-win deal, you are on the same side, not battling each other. Synergies come together, people come together, and a happy seller may provide real value, now that they're liberated from "running" a business.

D. Systems

Three primary advantages are offered here. First, you get their systems and they get yours, the best of the best. Second, with a larger company you have the capacity to put in more and better systems, because you may have better people, with more time who can create more systems. Third, after the transition, you will have time to do this.

9.   Location, location, location

This is the old mantra for retail and real estate, and it applies to other industries as well. There may be a particular location you want and can't get. It could be a retail location, and it could be, for manufacturers and distributors, a building near a distribution center, on a rail line, or close to suppliers. While this may not be a singular reason to make an acquisition, when combined with some of the other reasons it may be your tipping point. More apropos for most companies is to expand geographically by buying a similar business (competitor) in another market, i.e., a new location.

One of my clients purchased a California business similar to his Seattle company. His new business gives him added volume and the opportunity for faster growth, and he was able to hire an industry friend to be the chief California salesperson. The acquired firm had no sales team, as the owners, in their seventies, weren't active; they were "coasting."

10. Make a competitor go away

Some businesses have more than general industry competition; they have a specific competitor that stands in their way. It may be a fierce rival (along the lines of such bitter sports rivalries as the Steelers and

Bengals or the Yankees and Red Sox). Or there may simply not be a big enough market for either firm to break away from the other.

Acquire your competitor (or merge, if you're friendly). This may make fast growth easier, cheaper, and more achievable. It may allow for faster moves into other markets or segments using traditional growth strategies. This strategy ties in very well with the previous strategy of expanding geographically by acquisition. Keep in mind: if the rivalry is too bitter, there isn't much hope of a deal.

11. Psychology—be part of a winning team

Employees want to be part of a winning team. They want to feel they're contributing to a winning effort. It's very much like sports: the more the team wins, the greater the number of fans it has.

I'm thinking of a family friend, young man in his early twenties. He took a while to figure out some things in life, but he is now steadily employed and has been for the last few years (with the same company). He is proud of his job and his contribution to the company, and he showed disdain when a new, younger employee (whom he called "the kid") flaunted the rules and wasn't dedicated. (But let's be honest: some employees at this level don't care, but they're not the ones who are important anyway, like "the kid.")

Now elevate this to the more experienced people, including the management team. In one company there was some doubt about the general manager accepting new ownership. However, this doubt was unfounded, as he has leaped at the chance to execute quality controls, better processes, and accountability.

As mentioned above, when you create a breath of fresh air, the employees will want to be part of it.

12. Risk—it's a lot lower

John decided to grow his company into another market and did so by "starting" a new branch. Other than maintaining his existing vendor relationships, everything was new. But John wasn't able to manage the remote location as well as his home location (small businesses need "adult supervision"), and within a couple years he was in big trouble. This led him having to divest his home location to pay the debts of his startup.

Now, imagine that John had acquired a company selling similar products (in a remote market). Given all of the other 18 reasons in this chapter, it becomes evident that his risk would have been greatly reduced.

13. Overhead the same, volume higher

Look at all of the strategies above and below. Ninety percent or more of the time you will add volume without adding (all of) the corresponding overhead. This is often one of the prime motivators for making an acquisition. If, say, you have 40 employees and two staff accountants, and the other firm has 25 employees and two staff accountants, you will likely need only three staff accountants after the acquisition. Boom! One salary, tax, and benefit package goes to the bottom line. Or, as in the story about Fred, he was able to hire an accountant versus a bookkeeper. The same can happen with rent, other staff, phone, Internet, advertising, and more.

A client of mine once bought one of his suppliers, which was a small business with a lot of inefficiencies. My client was able to move his business into his supplier's space, replace at least one production worker (my client had capacity), and coordinate marketing efforts with no increase in marketing costs. In addition, just think of all of the other overhead my client could eliminate: telephone lines, accounting services, utilities, etc. He took a sleepy little company and turned almost all of its gross profit into pure net profit.

14. Synergy

In an oversimplified example, you sell paper, and the company down the street sells envelopes. You sell to the same customer base. Wouldn't it make sense for one salesperson, not two, to call on each customer and sell paper and envelopes? The same holds true for delivery people, warehouse people, and accounting (one monthly invoice, not two).

These situations don't come up every day. Savvy owners are always on the lookout for them, though. It need not be as blatant an example as paper and envelopes. This is one reason why my friend Fred jumped on his second acquisition even though it was sooner than he had preferred. He can now easier market multiple services without much extra effort or cost. (I've used Fred's acquisitions numerous times, because it's such a good example, and it's fresh in my mind.)

15. Technologies

I remember talking with a gate agent for Delta Airlines immediately after they bought Northwest Airlines (affectionately known as North Worst Airlines). I asked how the merger was going, and she made two comments. The first had to do with Delta's customer service strength, which Northwest lacked. (As a frequent Northwest flyer I could attest to that.)

The second statement was about how Northwest had some of the best technology in the industry and would immediately upgrade Delta's technology.

Find a company with the enterprise resource planning (ERP) system you wish you had, or with the automated processes and cloud access you desire so all offices are "live" all the time.

16. Vendor relationship strategies

Diversifying vendors means accessing ones you can't get on your own. Many have territories and protect their distributors and retailers. Acquiring one of their customers gets you in the door. Once there, you can make the most of the opportunity.

All of this assumes you're buying a company with different products than yours. This also works for buying a competitor (or similar business in another market) with the same product line. For retailers, this means buying a store that carries the same lines you carry. The result in either case is that you will do higher volumes with your suppliers and qualify for greater (volume) discounts.

The icing—the big three

Now here are the top three reasons to grow by acquisition.

17. Customers (efficiency vs. make more calls)

"This would be a great business if it wasn't for those darn customers" was a semiserious comment someone made to me years ago. He was referring to the annoying (bad) customers. It's good customers we all want more of—customers who are loyal, steady, in good financial shape and growing, and who pay their bills on time, appreciate the value you offer, and consider you part of their team.

I mentioned above that acquiring a new product or service line you can sell to your customers is a good reason for an acquisition. The same holds true for selling your current offerings to a new group of customers. Often this can be done without any increase in your sales force (actually sales forces, if you consider the salespeople with the acquired firm).

In an ideal situation, some products overlap between businesses, so some continuity and synergy will be achieved. (The figure below shows this.) Your salespeople now have an easy transition to discuss-

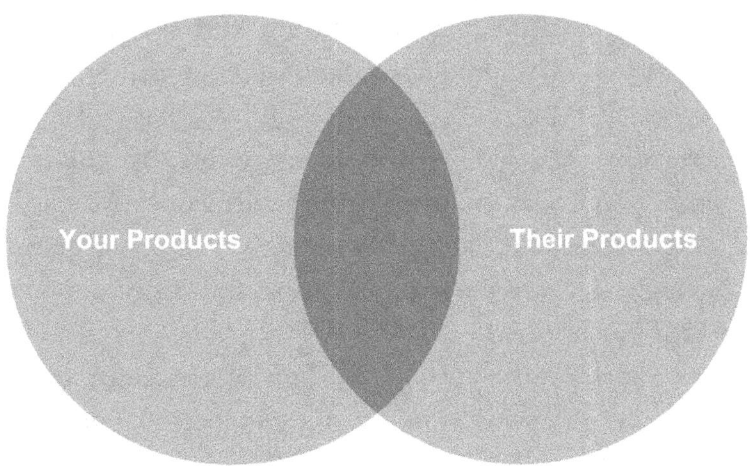

ing and selling, their products; likewise, their salespeople have an easy transition to discussing and selling yours.

Fundamentally, if your primary motivation is to acquire a customer base, you are acquiring market share. You may have many other reasons (above), but the bottom line is you are buying customers, and that means top-line growth.

18. Yes, we can!

This is not about ego; it is about building an exit strategy to get a higher selling price. Buying another company, assimilating it into your operation, and showing that the combined profits are greater than the two individual companies' profits demonstrates to potential buyers that this can be done. It proves you have the team that can integrate one operation into another.

This integration could involve their assimilation of your firm into theirs, or it could be a signal that growing your business (or, now, a division of theirs) is possible through further acquisitions. A management team that can successfully integrate other firms without major disruption and with immediate efficiencies is a valued team. Too many big mergers and acquisitions fail. Up to 95 percent of public mergers do not live up to expectations. A savvy buyer will appreciate this talent and experience associated with past integrations.

Keith bought a small manufacturing business that made a handful of proprietary products. The business was overly dependent on the seller, his products, and manufacturing skills. And it was marginally profitable, meaning there were small profits after paying the owner a fair-market salary for his work. Ultimately, it was a great deal for both sides. This was Keith's second acquisition, after buying a decades-old manufacturing and distribution company three years prior.

His second acquisition was one of the suppliers for the distribution side of his company. He knew the product, its potential, its weaknesses, and ways to sell more of it than the seller was doing.

This acquisition was also part of his overall exit strategy, as it showed he could purchase a company, absorb it into his operation profitably, and increase his rate of return on assets and sales.

For the seller, Keith was a lifesaver. Who else would buy a company so dependent on the owner's product development skills and product knowledge? Surely not an individual wanting to own her own business, nor another company with no insight into the product and its markets. In addition, the seller got a consulting job with Keith to engineer the products he had invented and those Keith's company had already made.

19. The bigger you are...the better

The bigger your business is, the more it will sell for, all other things being equal. A $50 million (revenue) company with 10 percent EBITDA will sell for a higher multiple of profit, EBITDA, free cash flow, or whatever metric you use than a $25 million company with 10 percent EBITDA, which will sell for a higher multiple than a $10 million company, and so on.

Companies with sales of $5 million to 50 million have historically sold for four to seven times EBITDA, while those on the higher end of EBITDA sold for the higher end of the multiple range. Grow your $5 million company to $15 million, and your multiple may increase by one times EBITDA (from 4 to 5, for example). Assuming 10 percent profit (and a 4 multiple), you can see the price go from $2 million to $7.5 million (10 percent profit at 5 times).

The fastest, safest way to grow from $5 million to 15 million is by acquisition. Buy another firm in your industry—a supplier, customer, or unrelated company that provides diversification—for an immediate revenue increase, a larger platform from which to grow organically, and more profit and a higher multiple when you exit.

"It's not bragging if you can do it." (Dizzy Dean, 1934)

Many business owners talk about their company's potential or the growth that will occur if the buyer just "does some marketing." Most of this is just talk. Business buyers of all types and sizes are a skeptical lot. When they hear too much about potential, they think the seller has tried every conceivable way to grow and can't.

Prove you can do it. Grow organically, and go out and buy another company. Show that you can integrate the people, processes, financial systems, customer service, and everything else into your operation. Private equity groups and large corporations make multiple acquisitions. If you can buy another firm and assimilate it, you become more attractive to these buyers. They will assume you can do it again and your management team is capable. Strategic buyers and equity group buyers highly value management teams, because they can even increase the multiple, compared to having the same size company that has not made acquisitions.

We have just covered 19 reasons why it makes sense to grow by acquisition. I realize that most of them don't apply to your business. It's the few that **do** apply that are the reasons why this strategy may make sense. Heck, your catalyst may be a reason not mentioned here. The point is, this has worked for many companies, and you should always have your eyes open for opportunities, as there are a lot of good reasons to do so.

At the same time, I must acknowledge that there are pitfalls you need to avoid, but they can be avoided if handled correctly. How you handle the cultural integration makes a huge difference. Letting (most of) the employees of both companies know their jobs are safe is important, as with any acquisition. And you will be taking on debt, but, as mentioned above, this debt comes with good things: customers, good margins, cash flow, etc. If it makes sense to buy another company, these pitfalls are easily overcome.

Due-Diligence Questionnaire

Buyers use this list judicially. If you are making an asset purchase, you are not buying the whole company (which is a stock sale), and you may not need many of the legal documents (check with your attorney). Trying to get all of this information will overwhelm any seller, and the smaller the business the greater the chances of the seller being overwhelmed.

Sellers realize that this is what buyers will ask. Most importantly, sellers need to get involved in conversations about the business and these topics. (Simply getting written answers won't help either buyer or seller nearly as much.)

Establish Responsibilities and Timeline First Legal Documents

- Is the corporation (or LLC) in good standing? Articles of incorporation

- Foreign jurisdictions: officers/directors/owners, subsidiaries and/or affiliates

- Special shareholder rights, i.e., preemptive rights or other agreements

- Minutes of board meetings (3 years) and by-laws

- What capital has been invested or loaned to business?

- How has the company been capitalized up till now?

Company's Business

- Describe the nature of the business.

- Describe each line of products and services sold.

- Describe the proposed emphasis and direction of the business.

- Is there an intention to widen the range of products and services sold?

- Are there any limitations to products, tariffs, licenses, copyrights, intellectual property trademarks, trade names, copyrights, patents, software, trade secrets, etc.?

- Describe the method of sales and the contracts with suppliers

- Describe the contracts with other companies

- Are subcontractors used? For what purpose?

- Are there any long-term contracts with subcontractors, etc.? (Include a list of competitors and a description of their products.)

- What do you know about the competitors' financing and technical resources?

- What is the ease or difficulty to enter this business? (Describe in detail.)

- Copies of technical information: trademarks, trade names, copyrights, licenses, etc.

- Copies of any major contracts

- Description of distribution channels

Industry Growth

- What is the estimated growth rate of the industry in the next five (5) years?

- What factors will affect growth in the future? Are industry-wide prices stable or increasing?

Marketing Strategy

- What are the marketing objectives?

- How will the objectives be put to use?

- What marketing effort is required?

- What expense is projected?

- How many people are involved in marketing?

- Who are these people, and how are they involved?

- What are historical sales increases/decreases by line (percentages)? (Include sales projections by product and by percentage of future revenue.)

Product Pricing

- How are products and services priced?

- Will there be any price changes in the future?

- How does pricing compare with competitive and comparable products? (Review actual invoices with major customers to check for discounts, special deals, etc.)

Customer Analysis

- Who are the customers?

- What are the trends in this customer group? (Make a customer list by volume of sales within the last three (3) years.)

- What is the procedure to sell products and services? (Include copies of all client agreements or contracts.)

- What will be the determining factors for a buying decision?

- Are sales controlled by a few high-priced, well-connected salespeople?

Facilities Required

- What facilities changes will be required in the future? (Include facility sizes and descriptions, as well as technology requirements such as hardware, software, licensing agreements, etc.)

Employees

- List of officers, directors, and other key employees

- Resumes of officers, directors, and other key employees

- List of all employees, their salaries, their dates of hire, and their job titles

- Copies of employment agreements

- Employee turnover: Is it out of the ordinary, or normal?

- Compensation schedule for owners, officers and key employees, including bonus plans

Due-Diligence List

- List of shareholders and their percentages of ownership in the company

- Company's attorney, CPA, insurance broker, health insurance broker, etc.

- Company's bank name(s), bank statements, deposit books, check register, QuickBooks files, etc.

- Environmental reports

- Employee manuals

- Copies of company leases

- List of all current major assets and their fair-market values

- Brochures and other marketing materials

- Annual financial statements of the last five (5) years

- Monthly financial statements of the last 1-2 years

- Accounts receivable aging report

- List of all debts and liabilities

- Copies of federal income tax returns for the last five (5) years (4506 with IRS, if needed)

- Copies of state sales and other state tax returns for the last 3-5 years

- Copies of all agreements, loan agreements, notes, pledge agreements, and security

- Copies of all profit-sharing or deferred compensation plans

- Company business plan

- Litigation history and anticipated (both ways), court search

- Insurance coverage and any changes to it

- Liens: equipment, tax, etc.

- Off-balance-sheet items, vacation, sick pay, etc.

- Proprietary information: drawings, reverse engineered and manufactured parts, etc.

About the Author

John Martinka is known as the Escape Artist because of the work he does in three areas:

1. Creating large exits for small businesses so the owner can leave the business with style, grace, and more money;

2. Helping executives escape the corporate world by buying the right business the right way;

3. Dramatically increasing the value of companies via growth by acquisition.

John has over 20 years of business experience as an intermediary, cofounded "Partner" On-Call Network, and has helped over 100 clients successfully navigate the treacherous waters of buy-sell transactions. He was awarded board approval in business acquisitions and sales by the Society for Advancement of Consulting, LLC. He currently serves on one for-profit company board and one non-profit board, and is very active with the Bellevue Breakfast Rotary Club.

In 2005, he started a Rotary project, "Improving Education through Technology," in conjunction with Cisco Networking Academy at Newport High School in Bellevue, Washington, to install computer labs in schools. As of this publishing, over 4,000 computers have been donated and installed in Slovakia, Turkey, and Antigua and Barbuda, with the students doing most of the onsite work.

The team has gone to Antigua 11 times to distribute 9,000 dictionaries to third-grade students, provide and install a video teleconferencing system between Antigua and Barbuda, and execute a program to train teachers on how to teach more effectively through technology. John's wife, Jan, has set up nine sewing centers in Antigua to teach women living in a high-poverty area the skill of sewing, which they use to make their families' clothes, school uniforms, and items to sell.

John's other books are:

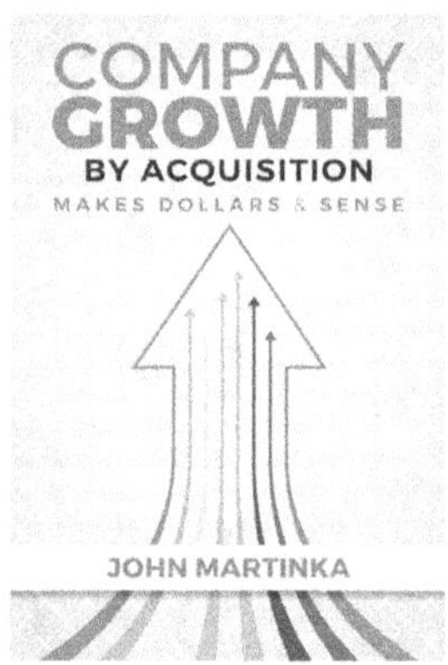

Learn more about John and his services at
www.martinkaconsulting.com.

You can reach him at john@johnmartinka.com
or 425-576-1814.